PROPER WORDS IN PROPER PLACES

PROPER WORDS IN PROPER PLACES

Writing To Inform

By

PAUL I. RICHARDS, Ph.D.

and

IRVING T. RICHARDS, Ph.D.

THE CHRISTOPHER PUBLISHING HOUSE
BOSTON, U.S.A.

To Our Wives,
whose suggestions and forbearance
have both been most helpful in this
and other endeavors.

". . . to consider what ought to be written and after what manner, he must first think and excogitate his matter, then choose his words, and examine the weight of either. Then take care, in placing and ranking both matter and words, that the composition be comely; and to do this with diligence and often. . . . seek the best, and be not glad of the forward conceits or first words that offer themselves to us; but judge of what we invent, and order what we approve."

BEN JONSON
(1573-1637)

CONTENTS

I. Theme and Overview 9

PART I — STRATEGY

II. The Reader's Problems 17

III. Guide The Reader 26

IV. Be Explicit 42

V. Reaching The Reader 61

PART II — MECHANICS

VI. The Shuffle Draft — How To Start 89

VII. Grammatical Commentary 107

VIII. Punctuation 146

IX. Troubleshooting 170

APPENDIX

Author and Printer 183

Proofreaders' Marks 198

Index 201

Proper Words in Proper Places

I

THEME AND OVERVIEW

Why does anyone write anything? Communication is the only conceivable purpose of writing, and a writer, although he should please himself, is really writing to his readers and for his readers. This remains true whether the writing is done as a chore, as a duty, as a pastime, or as a labor of love. In each case, nothing of significance will be accomplished until some reader grasps the writer's thought. Up to that moment, the words are mere blots on clean paper.

This book attempts to set forth the simple principles of using language to convey thoughts in print. If our discussions occasionally seem long, it is not because the principles are complicated but because their ramifications are extensive. Moreover, because language is not entirely logical, even a fundamentally simple principle may require considerable discussion and illustration before its full meaning has been made clear.

To simplify the discussion, the book has been intentionally confined to writing that is intended to explain something — to present arguments or observations. Perhaps this limitation can be made clearer by comparing the main types of written communication.

Writing can be divided approximately into two general classes, corresponding to two interwoven but rec-

9

ognizably different activities of a human mind — receiving sensations and creating thoughts: feeling and reflecting. Although these two activities may sometimes merge, sharing them with other minds requires, in general, correspondingly different techniques. The literature of the senses and emotions is descriptive or narrative, and its method is largely one of suggestion. The literature of thought is expository or argumentative, and its method is one of explicit statement.

To the extent that these types of writing sometimes merge, or to the extent that they have common requirements, this book concerns both. But literary writing, as we shall occasionally call the literature of the senses, seems to require an inborn sensitivity and a talent for artistic construction, such as knowing what to elaborate and what to omit. Such writing can convey extraordinarily subtle insights by imparting to the reader actual experiences and sensations — the concrete evidence from which the insights sprang. When fully successful, it stimulates in the reader the same sensuous, emotional, or imaginative reactions that the writer experienced, and these reactions then arouse in the reader the same insights they aroused in the writer. This book does not pretend to treat the subtleties of such techniques.

Expository writing, as we shall call the literature of facts and thought, is a much less nebulous, more direct task: one need only lay out the pertinent observations and arguments in an orderly fashion and in explicit words that do not twist or obscure the ideas they were intended to convey. Even this task presents a surprisingly difficult challenge, and the remainder of this book concerns suggestions for meeting that challenge.

It is sometimes said that if readers can understand

a work, it is well written. Whether this is a truth or a mere rationalization depends on the interpretation placed upon the word "understand." Merely that a given sample of writing can be uniquely decoded certainly does not mean that it is well written. Requesting extra effort from a reader is so unnecessary that writing cannot be labelled "good" unless an average reader can grasp the thought smoothly and effortlessly while reading along at a steady, even pace. If he must reread a sentence or pause to recognize the structure or intended meaning of groups of words, he has been put to unnecessary trouble, and the writing is correspondingly poor.

Scientific writing, perhaps the epitome of expository writing, amply illustrates both the challenge of clear writing and, too frequently, its difficulty. Almost all scientific effort necessarily ends in some sort of written report, which is usually the sole surviving tangible evidence of what was accomplished. But such reports are too often either confusing or tantalizingly inexpressive. Scientific records even include several important contributions that were originally ignored, merely because they were announced in terms unfamiliar or unclear to the readers who should have been most interested.

A scientist *is* what he writes. His writing is his public self. The truly outstanding men of any generation are known far more widely through their writings than through personal contacts. Although the quality of their research primarily determines their renown, no professional man can afford to befog his own efforts by vague, inexpressive reporting. If a scientist or engineer does not set forth his work so lucidly that even casual readers will perceive what was accomplished, its value and quality remain partly concealed. Despite such strong motivations, even technical writers too often lose some readers and fail to impart their full message to others.

Ensuring that few readers will miss or misinterpret a written message requires both care and planning, partly because writing is a secondary, derivative form of language. Speech, the form in which language develops and is most used, includes so many tonal modulations and other signals, all impossible to transcribe, that a large part of the writer's task is to avoid carrying over to his writing many unconscious habits that he has acquired in speech.

The writer must remember that each reader reads by himself — that reading is a silent, solitary, one-way process. Correspondingly, the writer's primary job is to help his readers by anticipating their individual, solitary reactions to his words. In daily conversation, few of us are surprised or offended when a listener asks for further details, confesses puzzlement, or betrays misunderstanding. When the speaker becomes a writer and the listener a reader, such problems are greatly magnified, partly because the printed words have lost the tonal modulations and other subtleties of speech, and partly because the reader cannot request amplification or clarification. Since he is alone with a mere transcript of the writer's words, he must extract what meaning he can from the words as they stand — or rather, he will extract as much meaning as he feels is worth his effort.

If the writer does not carefully smooth the reader's path by anticipating and forestalling as many confusions, delays, and misunderstandings as he can, the very purpose of his writing may be defeated, partially if not completely. Nothing significant is gained when the words "sound" well to the writer; he himself is not likely to misunderstand them, and he cannot later declaim them to his readers. It is the reader, scanning the words in silence and in solitude, who must respond if anything of importance is to be accomplished. If some readers unnecessarily misinterpret, lose interest, or fail to discover parts of the message, the writer's efforts have been correspondingly wasted.

HELP THE READER is the one inviolable rule of writing. Occasionally, it may even justify violating any other rule. Most of the remainder of this book consists of suggestions for helping the reader. The subject, of course, is vast, and no set of suggestions can be in any way exhaustive, a situation that we have attempted to ameliorate by confining the discussion to expository writing, as previously explained. Yet even our limited discussion probably encompasses too much material to be absorbed properly in one reading.

Accordingly, we suggest to our reader that the most practical way to use this book is to choose from it two or three points that seem to him especially cogent or potentially effective. If his attempts to employ these particular suggestions appear profitable, he should perhaps wait until they have become habits before returning to choose several more for similar testing. As with any art worth learning, he cannot ever hope to be completely satisfied with his writing skill, or indeed, with any single product of his efforts. But if the problems of writing truly capture his interest, he will find that occasional insights and flashes of ingenuity can be as gratifying in this endeavor as in any other.

PART I

STRATEGY

II

THE READER'S PROBLEMS

To help the reader, it is essential to understand the sources of his difficulties and annoyances. Many of the reader's problems are subconscious, at least to the extent that he often cannot explain in detail what troubles him or why a particular paper seems long-winded, unclear, or difficult. Virtually the entire craft of good writing can be summarized in the command, "Help the reader," but this injunction can be effective only if the writer understands the origin and nature of the reader's inarticulate needs.

We are not, of course, discussing any insurmountable, impenetrable barriers to communication, which a sufficiently determined, sympathetic reader could not overcome. Rather, we shall be considering unnecessary annoyances and avoidable distractions, which may accumulate to a greater or lesser degree. No writing is entirely free of them, but good writing is characterized by their rarity. The fewer the distractions and temporary confusions, the larger will be the portion of the reader's attention that can be devoted to the message, and the larger will be the number of readers who do not lose interest.

An analogy may help to clarify the relationship between the writer and his readers. Consider a competent, well-constructed lecture that is delivered in a very heavy foreign accent. A portion of each hearer's mind must be devoted to "translating" the unfamiliar sounds and strangely used words into idiomatic English. Following the thoughts of such a lecturer is hard work, particularly if his message is not simple.

As a result of this demand for additional effort, such a lecturer is actually followed carefully only by hearers who either have a strong sympathy for him or have been led (by his reputation, perhaps) to expect that the effort will be especially rewarding. If the lecturer is unknown, the proportion of his audience that make an effort sufficient to grasp what he is saying may actually be very small.

A heavy foreign accent, in short, is no asset, and its possessor is only prudent when he makes an effort to divest himself of this impediment to communication. Perhaps he cannot hope for perfection, but this is no reason for neglecting to attempt at least some improvement. Similarly, a writer (even a good writer) is only prudent to strive constantly to remove any impediments that may distract a reader or make unnecessary demands upon him.

The analogy must be abandoned at this point, since the source and nature of the distractions in the two situations are different, even though their net effects are similar. To develop a strategy for eliminating the reader's problems, it is expedient to consider some aspects of the reader's precise situation.

READING IS SOLITARY. A paper confronts each reader individually. When a reader takes up the paper, he is alone with an inanimate array of printed symbols, which will neither reply to his spontaneous questions nor respond in any way to his mood or attitude. These conventionalized ink blots are all that the reader has to work with, and his only recourse is to look at them in silence.

READING IS ONE-WAY. Despite a certain figurative truth in such phrases as "communing with the author," the literal facts are that the writer is not present and that ideas can flow only from the printed symbols into the reader's mind. Nothing can flow in the opposite direction. If the reader is puzzled, he can only reread the same words, stop, or pass on, hoping for later clarification. If he misinterprets a passage, only an apparent contradiction in a later passage can warn him that he has misunderstood. There is no way he can test his interpretations or request clarifications. There can be no give and take.

READING IS STRICTLY VISUAL. The reader must use his sense of sight, and only his sense of sight, to understand words, sentences, and language. Language developed, however, primarily in speech, and speech is its primary use. That comprehending speech is fundamentally different from reading is perhaps best shown by the fact that the one is soon learned effortlessly by all normal human beings, whereas the other requires extensive formal training. Even though reading becomes a subconscious skill after long practice, it remains a rather unnatural, inherently complex process, in which only the eye can be used, although the ear is the natural avenue of our language.

READING VERSUS LISTENING

We seldom stop to consider that everyday speech contains many signals in addition to words. Even a formal lecturer conveys to his audience occasional connotations and attitudes that disappear completely in a stenographic transcript of his words. Extemporaneous discussion loses far more in a literal transcript, which is invariably confusing and often nearly unintelligible (a fact that seems to have escaped the editors of some conference proceedings).

It is illuminating to examine some of the speech signals that a hearer subconsciously perceives but that are lost in a printed record of mere words. Perhaps the most important nonverbal signals are emphasis and speed of delivery. Consider almost any simple sentence, such as,

I will call at your office.

or, more dramatic,

I never said he stole money.

When these are said without emphasis, with a lowered tone of voice and a rapid delivery, they carry a rather noncommittal meaning that approximates the meaning a reader would usually receive. When either example is spoken aloud several times, however, with heavy emphasis on a different word each time (*I* will call . . . , I *will* call . . . , I will *call* . . . , etc.), then an entirely different set of meanings emerges. These meanings cannot be conveyed with these words in print (except by italics, which quickly lose their force if repeated too frequently). In speech, vague, imprecise words can be given a wide variety of specific meanings through relative emphasis and speed of delivery. Colloquialisms are often highly expressive in conversation but are usually quite lifeless in print.

Tone of voice or deliberate pauses may even distinguish formal word meanings. A derisive, or apologetic, or serious tone of voice can indicate the particular sense in which an otherwise colorless or ambiguous word is to be understood. In day-to-day discussion a speaker will often start, "From the way you said that, you obviously meant . . . ." He is explicitly stating that a nonverbal signal was made and interpreted.

Grammatical structure may also be indicated by emphasis or speed of delivery. A parenthetic phrase is usually uttered in a lower tone of voice, with little emphasis and a delivery more rapid than the main clause. If a grammatical interruption is especially long, the return to the main clause may be indicated by a pause or by heavy emphasis on the first few words of the continuation. If, as often happens in everyday speech, a grammatical structure must be abandoned, the speaker may sigh, make a grimace, or take a conspicuously deep breath.

Other signals come readily to mind now that we have belabored emphasis and delivery. Even a formal lecturer may indicate a grammatical parenthesis by a gesture, such as a lowering of the head or a sweep of the hand. In personal conversation, gestures can be more subtle and more frequent. Facial expressions become important, those of the listener as well as those of the speaker. The speaker watches his listener's face (to some extent subconsciously) and adjusts his later statements in accordance with what he judges the listener's reactions to be. He may even stop and retrace previous statements in response to these "feedback" signals from a silent listener.

In day-to-day speech even visual or social context can supply missing information. If a man announces, "I have an immature personality," his hearer will interpret this in different ways depending on whether the speaker is (a) a psychiatric patient, (b) a guest at a cocktail party, or (c) a personnel manager pointing to someone's filled-out application blank. The sentence could be rephrased to express only one of these meanings, but in day-to-day speech this would not be necessary. Usually the hearers would not even notice any alternative meanings, unless the delivery and tone of voice were deliberately humorous.

Not only do nonverbal signals carry much of the information in speech, but conversely, the words themselves are sometimes made intentionally uninformative. Children quickly learn to use simple syllables, "uh . . . er . . . ," to indicate that they wish to say something but have not yet arranged it in words. Similarly, adults acquire a store of neutral, sentence-starting phrases that convey little or no information but serve to hold the listener while thoughts are being organized. ("In regard to that question, my position would be that . . . I . . . .") From the delivery and lack of emphasis, the listener recognizes such phrases for what they are, and he politely waits, meanwhile largely discounting the words he is hearing.

SILENT WORDS

Returning to the reader's problems, we see why writing, which contains only words, cannot literally duplicate everyday speech. It is simply *impossible* to "write the way you talk"; a reader sees only the words. Of course, a few unvoiced signals are used in writing. Punctuation indicates grammatical structure to some extent, and paragraphing usually signals some change in thought.

But these visual signals are poor substitutes for the prolific nonverbal signals of speech. Only the question mark, exclamation point, period, and capital letter have relatively unambiguous, though general, meanings. Upon the inconspicuous little comma falls almost the entire burden of indicating grammatical structure within a sentence, and this duty is so onerous that the comma must be reserved for this purpose alone. Any attempt to employ punctuation in ways not sanctioned by usage can only confuse the reader. Stress can occasionally be indicated by italics, but experience has shown that italics lose their effectiveness unless they are reserved for rare instances where they are absolutely indispensable.

It is equally important to realize that the reader has learned (perhaps subconsciously) to use the few signals that are available. Compare *I will call at your office, and* . . . with *I will call at your office and* . . . . The signal *(, and)* leads a reader to expect a second independent clause, complete with subject, verb, and object, but the signal *(and)* leads him to anticipate a second verb, sharing the original subject, *I* (or perhaps a second noun, as object of *at*).

Again, note that the following two sentences have slightly different meanings:

> *The knife that is on the shelf has been sharpened.*
> *The knife, which is on the shelf, has been sharpened.*

The first identifies a particular knife (by specifying its location) and then states that it has been sharpened. The second assumes that a particular knife has already been identified (by context, presumably) and, after incidentally mentioning its present location, states primarily that it has been sharpened. Preserving the distinction between the signals *(that)* and *(, which)* is surprisingly helpful, even to readers who are not consciously aware of any distinction.

The point of these examples is not so much that a missing comma or ambiguous word might distort the meaning of a passage. Context would usually restore the sense. Rather, the point is that such ineptitudes may temporarily mislead the reader. He must then revise his expectations and perhaps glance back to recapture the intended sense. Annoyances of this sort need not be especially frequent to exasperate an unsympathetic reader, even though he may not be conscious of precisely what makes the writing seem vague and disorganized.

The main essentials of the reader's problems, then, can be summarized as follows:

(1) Communication is entirely one-way. The reader cannot ask questions, and if he misinterprets, he cannot easily be warned. If he is puzzled, he can only reread the very words that puzzle him, or pass along, hoping for later clarification.

(2) He must accept language in a derivative form. Reading is unavoidably more taxing than listening. Part of the mind is necessarily employed in translating visual symbols into words and is unavailable for thinking about the message.

(3) Written language is merely a transcript of the writer's words. Any subconscious pattern of relative stress that the writer may have intended has disappeared, and can be reconstructed only if it is essentially unique and therefore uninformative. Word meanings may thereby have become ambiguous or even altered.

As a general rule, the reader is most likely to be misled or inconvenienced by:

(1) Grammatical relationships.
(2) The specific intended sense of words or phrases.

Clarifying these matters will not completely restore the full power of the same words used in speech, but the primary annoyances to a reader will be mitigated.

The next two chapters discuss some detailed implications of these two main avenues to the strategy of writing. In general, the writer's greatest difficulty is to avoid carrying over into his writing some of the habits he has acquired in speech, the more natural use of language. An effort of imagination is required to approach one's own writing with the unprepared eyes of one's readers, who must reconstruct the message out of the printed symbols alone.

III

GUIDE THE READER

If readers are not to be delayed or misled by grammatical misunderstandings, the grammar must be more than merely correct. It must be so clear and so immediately obvious that it is completely unobtrusive, and the reader need give it no thought. This quality is often what is meant by a "flowing style." The words fall into place so naturally, one after the other, that the reader feels as though they were flowing effortlessly through his mind. The effect is achieved primarily by eliminating grammatical constructions that, while technically correct, are clumsy and difficult to read at first glance.

Admittedly, few writers think consciously of grammar as they write. In practice, a writer usually thinks mainly of ideas and vocabulary until his inner ear warns him that a sentence is becoming confusing, or he may not notice the confusion until he later rereads what he has written. In either case, if he does not immediately perceive what is wrong, he can usually locate the ineptitude by at least a partial grammatical analysis. Be this as it may, such problems are fundamentally grammatical and must be discussed in grammatical terms.*

_____

* For a detailed discussion of grammar, see Chapter VII.

Habits

It may be helpful to consider first some sources of grammatical ineptitudes. Awkward constructions are more nearly the rule than the exception in extemporaneous speech. A casually started sentence frequently acquires subordinate clauses and phrases in profusion as the speaker recalls qualifications and subtopics that should be attached to his main thought. The result may even be ungrammatical, but no harm need be done, since the speaker usually knows whether he is understood. If the hearer's expression suggests confusion, the speaker will abandon his sentence in the middle and recast his entire statement.

Similarly, a writer may find that a sentence is becoming more and more complicated as he develops it or adds insertions and qualifications. Unfortunately, with the words laid out before him, he can often devise a few minor changes that will produce technically correct grammar. But the result will not be grammatical in the wider sense if it is unnecessarily complex and confusing. A writer should try to avoid carrying over into his writing the habit, natural in speech, of starting a sentence before he knows where it will lead. A sentence should be a "mindful" of thought; it should not contain more material than can be comfortably held in mind at one time.

Ungrammatical constructions, common as they may be in speech, should be avoided in writing, not just because they are undignified, but because they are unnecessary and will confuse the reader unless the sentence is very short. The reader will notice that the words he has read are ungrammatical, and thinking that he must have misread, he will waste time retracing the sentence to be sure of the words.

Some grammatical constructions can be perfectly clear in a formal lecture but nevertheless confusing to a reader. This is especially true of clauses interrupted by subordinate, qualifying, or incidental material. In speech, such interrupting, parenthetic remarks can be identified by a "throw away" oral delivery, but in writing, no such device is available, and the substitute devices (commas, dashes, parentheses) must be used sparingly lest their "profusion produce confusion." When interruptions are too frequent or too long, the proper pairing of the commas or parentheses is no longer visually obvious.

Accordingly, a writer should not attempt to convey relative patterns of stress to the reader. Especially, he should not try to indicate pauses or relative emphasis by punctuation. Punctuation has come to have the function of visually indicating grammatical structure, and experience has shown that it must be reserved for this purpose alone. Punctuation is for the reader, not some orator, and it must have the same meaning for all readers if it is to serve any purpose whatever. Certain "common law" rules of punctuation, already developed through experience and usage, have been subconsciously learned by the reader, and any departures can only confuse him.*

Some interruptions, of course, can be clearly indicated by standard punctuation and will cause the reader no difficulty. Common sense and discretion are the best guides in deciding whether an interruption

---

* Rules of punctuation are discussed at length in Chapter VIII.

will be confusing. As interruptions are made longer, they become more likely to give the reader trouble, and if words depend strongly upon one another (as in an idiom or a compound verb, for example), separating them even by a short interruption may obscure their relation. If a sentence is already complex enough to require considerable punctuation, interruptions that could be readily indicated in speech may require loading the sentence with an overburden of commas that the reader cannot quickly sort out.

Technical and other precise expository writing is particularly prone to complex, convoluted grammatical constructions, because a precise statement often requires extensive qualification for accuracy. A technical writer often finds that a previously written statement requires further qualifications, and there is frequently great temptation to pile insertion upon insertion. Beware of insertions, especially belated insertions. In any case, try to place extensive qualifications either in separate sentences or at least in grammatically separated form, either introducing or following the main statement.

As a general rule of common sense in all these matters, the longer the sentence, the clearer its grammatical structure should be. A short sentence inherently isolates its peculiarities from the surrounding material and focuses the reader's attention where he will need it.

Above all, remember the difference between sight-reading print and listening to speech. If a sentence requires certain mental modulations of tone when it is read, it is almost certain to delay many readers. Make the material easy to read, not easy to declaim.

INTERRUPTIONS

Let us turn now to a somewhat more explicit discussion of these general points. Interruptions require the reader to hold incomplete thoughts in mind, while absorbing other complete thoughts. Notice this effect in the example, *Such theories do not, because of their common assumptions, suffice for the problem at hand.* If the reader is merely asked to keep a subject in mind, the effect is somewhat less confusing: *Such theories, because of their common assumptions, do not suffice for the problem at hand.* But if the interruption is sufficiently long, even holding a simple subject in mind becomes annoying: *Such theories, because of their common assumptions and their reliance upon purely geometrical constructions and arguments, do not suffice for the problem at hand.* Both of the last two sentences are easier to read if the interruption is avoided completely: *Such theories do not suffice for the problem at hand because . . . .*

Particularly annoying to the reader is an avoidable interruption that is followed by nothing of significance: *Sirius is the brightest star (of magnitude − 1.6 and 8.73 light years away) in the heavens.* Here the reader is put to the trouble of bridging the parenthesis only to find that this effort draws a blank in the anticlimactic end of the sentence.

Mere rearrangement will not always clear up an awkward construction. For example: *This is one of the methods, if not the only method, which can measure the losses.* Changing *which* to *that* offers some help, but the interruption cannot be easily moved. Altering the construction, however, will clear up the sentence: *This is perhaps the only method that can measure the losses.* If the subsidiary idea is of crucial importance, give it a correspondingly important grammatical role: *This method can measure the losses; indeed, it may be the only method that can.*

Sometimes the structure must be altered to convert compound interruptions into simple interruptions: *In some aspects of the study, the properties of specific molecules for example, it is found . . . .* The simple comma is powerless to indicate clearly that *for example* is a parenthesis within a parenthesis. Rewording will avoid the difficulty: *In some aspects of the study, such as the properties of specific molecules, it is found . . . .* This form also prevents the reader from assuming that the first comma marks the end of the introductory phrase and that *the properties* is the main grammatical subject.

Eliminating long interruptions is part of a somewhat more general technique of "closing out the grammatical accounting." If each long thought is completed before the next is started, the reader can follow the sentence readily, even though it may be extremely long, and indeed, we wonder whether you, the reader, may have failed to notice that this very sentence is an example, a somewhat artificial example, since the material following the main conjunction was added merely to produce this effect.

The following, less artificial example shows that "grammatical closure" has more general application than merely avoiding long interruptions:

Smith's results support the view of the band theory of crystalline solids as a valid approach.

Changing only two words avoids the lengthy grammatical suspension:

> *Smith's results support the view that the band theory of crystalline solids is a valid approach.*

The reader need not hold the first five words in mind after passing *that.* The relief to his powers of concentration is almost as complete as it would be if the sentence were split into two independent sentences *(Smith's results support the following view. The band theory . . .* — a poor form, however, for so simple a thought).

Although occasional short interruptions are allowable and even provide pleasant variety of style, grammatically related words should not be separated unduly by interruptions. Splitting a compound verb or a common expression (such as *different from*) by a single adverb or a short phrase (*different in many ways from* or *has frequently occurred*) is not especially objectionable, but somewhat longer interrupting modifiers can only invite confusion (*has frequently in this connection occurred* or *different in two ways, arithmetic and geometric, from*).

Sometimes even a single inserted word is awkward: *Similar results to these were found by Jones.* Here, *similar to* is an idiom that should not be split; even in a short sentence the effect is awkward. The words can be rearranged to avoid the split: *Results similar to these were found by Jones.* Or the idiom can be eliminated: *Jones' results were similar.* If this seems too short, it can be combined with the sentence that follows it: *Comparing our finding with Jones' similar results, ...*

This last example suggests the reason for the abhorrence of the split infinitive that was recently current. The modern concensus holds, more sensibly, that a short split, such as a single adverb, is often no more objectionable than a similar short split of any other compound verb form. But split infinitives can easily become confusing and should be avoided when other arrangements will serve equally well. Long splits, of course, should be avoided not only in infinitives but also between any pair of closely related words.

PRUNING

In simplifying long sentences, another device (in addition to "grammatical closure") is to eliminate un-informative modifiers and shorten the remaining ones. Unnecessary modifiers are discussed in the next chapter. Adjectival phrases can often be replaced by adjectives, and adverbial phrases by adverbs:

> *of sufficient generality* means
>   *sufficiently general*
> *in the subsequent discussion* (often) means
>   *subsequently*
> *of a large size* means *large*

Similar elimination of "little words," with a consequent simplification of grammar, can sometimes be arranged by changing a noun to a participle or an infinitive:

> *for the determination of* X means
>   *for determining* X or *to determine* X
> *mechanism of removal of* X means
>   *mechanism for removing* X

Sometimes, words can be eliminated entirely (*which we expect to occur* means simply *which we expect*). Finally, subordinate clauses can often be replaced

by shorter grammatical forms, in particular by appositives, especially when the clause starts with *that
are . . . , which is . . . ,* or the like:

> *Knives that are sharp* means *sharp knives . . .*
> *. . . hydrogen, which is the lightest gas, . . .*
> means *. . . hydrogen, the lightest gas, . . .*
> *. . . the method that was effective . . .* means
> *. . . the effective method . . .*

In general, this device for shortening and simplifying
the elements of long sentences can be summarized as
an *attempt to eliminate prepositions and relative pronouns.* Naturally, prepositions and relative pronouns
have their proper uses, and such drastic measures are
usually needed only when the sentence seems basically
sound but nevertheless "wordy." A string of mono-
syllabic words usually indicates that this sort of treatment would be advisable.

On the other hand, do not abbreviate grammatical
structures. Notice, for example, that we did not recommend eliminating verbs, as such. Incomplete constructions tend to be confusing unless they are both
short and strictly parallel to an immediately preceding
construction. The writer's over-all goal is to guide
the reader smoothly through the grammar, and this
cannot be done by requiring him to supply missing
words. The sentence, *Complex electronic systems are
unreliable unless underrated* requires more attention
and time from the reader than: *Complex electronic
systems are unreliable unless the components are operated below normal ratings.* The longer form can be
read through in less time than it takes an average
reader to grasp the full meaning of the short, incomplete version.

Such telegraphic constructions spare the writer's wrist but not the reader's mind, and the full meaning intended by the writer may well be missed by his less interested readers. While long sentences can often be improved by *substituting* a short grammatical form for a long one, the reader is not helped when a structure is merely abbreviated to an incomplete form.

ALTERNATE READINGS

Grammatical ambiguities, our final category, are an inherent danger in any uninflected ("isolating") language. The grammatical roles of English words are not fixed; nouns may be used as adjectives (*machine translation* or *party politics*), and adjectives can be used as nouns (*in binary* or *the poor*); the present participle of a verb (". . . ing") may be used as an adjective or a noun. Thus, English often relies solely on word order to indicate grammatical roles, and if the modifiers are themselves modified, or if many modifiers refer to the same word, the reader may have difficulty untangling the grammatical structure.

Since the grammatical versatility of English words contributes much to the power of the language, any attempt to avoid grammatical ambiguities entirely would only weaken that power. Any hard and fast rules for eliminating the dangers would also eliminate the advantages. The writer must therefore rely almost entirely on his imagination to uncover alternate constructions that some readers might see in his words. In attempting to do this, the writer is in an especially difficult position, since his intended interpretation will usually seem to him the most natural one, if not the unique one. He must employ a lively imagination to discover alternative readings, and he must exercise a charitable regard for the reader's foibles in deciding whether to eliminate them.

In some cases, the meaning is essentially unique, and the only disadvantage is the reader's loss of time as he untangles the structure or else notes that the meaning is indeed invariant. A borderline example is *shock wave structure,* which may be read *shock-wave structure* or *shock wave-structure.* The two meanings are not very different, and the phrase is so short that it might be left standing when other forms would complicate other parts of the sentence. The rather extreme example *upper atmosphere reaction rate data are* . . . also has an unambiguous meaning but should definitely be changed, because the reader must scan three nouns, each time thinking that he has reached the true noun, only to find that it must have been an adjective. By the time he finally reaches *data,* he is either puzzled or exasperated.

In other cases, even the meaning of the words may change with the interpretation. Does *big business research* mean research funded by big business, research that is operated like a big business, or research on the operations of big business?

Another common form of grammatical ambiguity might be called the "double-edged modifier." Sometimes, word position suggests that the modifier refers to one word, whereas the sense requires that it refer to another. For example, *The gel has all the properties of a wire necessary to transmit transverse waves.* Only after the reader has passed several words beyond *necessary* does he realize that it cannot modify *wire* but must refer to *properties.* A similar example is, *With further training, the psychologist taught the mouse to discriminate shapes.*

Dangling modifiers are modifiers that clearly should have a grammatical referent but actually have no logically identifiable one. They often result from changing the construction of a sentence without recognizing that the referent of the modifier disappears at the same time. In addition to confusing the reader, dangling modifiers may produce unfortunate or humorous effects by appearing to modify some other nearby noun. *Holding the torch flame against the flange, solder is flowed into the joint.* (The illogical dangling participle should not be confused with the entirely logical "absolute construction," wherein the participle is a verb and has its own subject: *The torch flame being held against the flange, solder is flowed into the joint.*)

Somewhat akin to grammatical ambiguities are situations where the first reading may suggest an ungrammatical construction. Even though more careful examination may show that the grammar is technically correct, the construction should be changed to avoid delaying the reader. A frequent form of this difficulty arises when, for example, a plural noun falls between a verb and its singular subject. On first reading, the verb may seem not to agree with its subject, the first noun. Any possible difficulties of this sort can often be eliminated by making the nouns both plural or both singular. Thus, *Detailed examination of the equations shows* . . . might be misread but neither of the following can be: *Detailed studies of the equations show* . . . or *Detailed examination of the theory shows* . . . . (It is still true that some readers may take the second noun to be the subject of the verb, but the meaning is not significantly affected, and there is no delay.)

The best general rule is probably to make the necessary changes whenever there can be the slightest doubt about interpretation. No single construction is ever uniquely appropriate, and a good writer can always find many completely different ways to express the same thoughts. English is so rich in both vocabulary and grammatical devices that no writer can justifiably feel that his initial construction, or even his fifth construction, could not be replaced by another that is at least as clear. The goal is always to minimize the fraction of readers who may be delayed or annoyed, and this goal is usually best served by appropriate changes whenever any question arises, whether or not the changes seem really necessary.

SIMPLIFYING DEVICES

Several rather minor points should also be mentioned in any discussion of structural guidance for the reader:

The active voice uses simpler verb forms than the passive voice, and it places the object of the action in the natural position, after the verb.* Passive voice tends to be weak and hesitant, partly because the agent of the action need not be named, and perhaps because the construction is inverted, with the grammatical subject serving as "logical object" of the verb. For these reasons, active voice is usually preferable, but the point should not be insisted upon, since there are often good reasons for using the passive voice. Sometimes, naming the agent would distract attention from the central thought; sometimes, the "logical object" should be placed at the beginning of the sentence to provide a link to previous thoughts. Nevertheless,

---

* Active: *A plastic sleeve insulated the rotor.*
Passive: *The rotor was insulated by a plastic sleeve.*

a writer will often find that a stubborn sentence will simplify when recast into the active voice. A passive verb with a *by* . . . phrase (establishing the agent, of the action) often indicates that active voice would be simpler and clearer.

Partly for this reason, the "editorial we" has outlasted its pontifical origins to become a conventional device for simplifying grammatical structures. The pronoun *we* is admittedly illogical when a single author refers to his own acts, and it may be presumptuous when it includes the reader ("*We* conclude that . . ."). Nevertheless, the "editorial we" allows simple, direct grammatical constructions that are often unattainable in any other way. The impersonal pronoun, *one,* seldom used in speech, is stilted and distracting. Not only is it identical with the number *one,* but it also lacks the full inflections of *we, our, us,* and *ours.* The advantages of the "editorial we" so outweigh minor illogicalities that it has become an accepted device in English writing.

Parallelism, a correspondence between successive structures, probably derives much of its value from the aid that it offers the reader (or listener). The impression that it creates is one of balance or rhythm, and the very essence of rhythm is predictability. When a grammatical structure is repeated, the reader quickly senses the repetition, and the remaining words flow easily and naturally through his mind. Any similarity in the lengths or sounds of corresponding words heightens this effect and hastens its recognition. Since the device seems to be natural to most users of English, and since repetition is all too easily overdone, the subject should perhaps not be stressed unduly. We merely note that, when parallelism is used, it should be com-

plete.   For example, an infinitive phrase in parallel
with a participial phrase merely invites confusion.

It is also helpful to remember that paragraphing is a
visual device that primarily provides resting places for
the reader.   It is well to make each paragraph deal
with a single topic that is announced in the opening
sentence and, perhaps, summarized in the final sentence, but this rule should not be slavishly followed
when it would require unnatural interruptions in the
train of thought or when it would produce extremely
long paragraphs.   Unduly long paragraphs, in particular, should be broken up to avoid discouraging the
reader and to give him an occasional resting place.

Finally, although this chapter attempts to present
an organized discussion, it must be admitted that many
ineptitudes defy codification.   The example, *At that
time theorists had little to work with by way of concepts from what is now known as quantum chemistry*
is manifestly clumsy and difficult to read.   Yet, specific
faults are difficult to identify, and about all that can
be done is to recommend recasting the sentence completely.   For example, *At that time the modern concepts of quantum chemistry were not available.*   When
all is said and done, no discussion of grammatical
guidance can be complete.   The writer must rely on
his imagination and ingenuity to find and to correct
many peculiar difficulties that arise in forcing a living
language into printed symbols.

No matter how many specific suggestions a writer
may have adopted, he must occasionally fall back on
the general principle of good writing, HELP THE READER.
Insofar as grammatical guidance is concerned, the
main principles may be summarized as follows.

Grammar must be more than merely correct. It must be so unobtrusive that the reader need not think about the structure, need not supply missing words, and need not hold words in mind, waiting for their grammatical partners. The longer the sentence, the clearer its grammar must be. Grammatical interruptions and grammatical ambiguities are the most common sources of delay or annoyance.

IV

BE EXPLICIT

To help all readers understand the message, the writer must choose precise words. A vague or unnecessary phrase may not only conceal a point from some readers, but may also suggest to others an assertion that was not intended. To be clearly understood by as many readers as possible, writing must be "explicit" in all senses: definite, plainspoken, unambiguous; leaving nothing implied or disguised; clearly developed, with all parts expressed.

We leave to a later chapter those aspects of precision that concern over-all organization. This chapter is concerned with vocabulary and phraseology. It might seem strange that an entire chapter could profitably be devoted to such matters, but again, we shall see that a writer must constantly combat certain natural habits acquired in speech.

Since speech takes place in time, many of its conventions stem from a tacit requirement that the words flow at a certain minimal rate. Various social circles recognize various polite devices for gaining time to think ahead, but every social context places a limit on the maximum allowable delay, after which the listener feels free to direct his attention elsewhere. The writer, of course, is bound by no such convention, since the reader's rate of progress is unrelated to the time taken to compose the words. Unconscious habits, however, may interfere with taking full advantage of this fact.

Vacuous constructions in speech, as mentioned in Chapter II, appear to serve primarily the purpose of holding a listener's attention. Not only are such phrases unnecessary in writing, but worse yet, because the monotone delivery is lost in print, they may divert the reader's attention from the true, logical content of the sentence. *In print, nothing shows the reader which of the words carry the thought and which were merely set down semiconsciously, while the writer was searching for the important ones.*

The reader naturally assumes that the main clause of a sentence carries the main thought and that each subordinate clause or phrase was inserted for some purpose. Indeed, he cannot very well proceed on any other assumption, just as a person listening to unvaried, absolutely monotone speech would be forced to consider each word carefully if he wished to grasp the thought.

Vacuous Constructions

In the light of these observations, consider the following example. *A computer program is often written that must deal with a problem having several variations.* The main thought is contained in the first three and last three words. The main verb *is written* conveys no useful information whatever. Its adverb *often* expresses a qualification, which, however, is easily obtained without the verb: *Many computer programs must deal with problems having several variations.* Or, more precisely: *Many computer programs must include several variations.*

A particularly common vacuous construction is illustrated by, *There are many X that* .... Except in rare instances, where the existence of X is vital to the dis-

cussion and must be asserted, this construction is simply equivalent to: *Many X . . . .*
Similar phrases, usually of this nature, are:

> *It is interesting that . . .*
> (Delete)
> *The results one has in these experiments . . .*
> *(These results . . .)*
> *Some authors are frequently inclined to . . .*
> *(Authors often . . .)*
> *X's are useful because they . . .*
> *(X's . . .)*
> *Experiments have been performed that show . . .*
> *(Experiments show . . .)*
> *This is a difficulty that . . .*
> *(This difficulty . . .)*
> *At the time when . . .*
> *(When . . .)*
> *Because of the fact that . . .*
> *(Because . . .)*
> *Under circumstances such that . . .*
> *(When . . .)*

Not all vacuous phrases occur at the beginning of a sentence or contain its main verb. For example, *. . . from the point of view of determining whether . . .* means no more than *. . . for determining whether . . .* or *. . . to determine whether . . . .* Again, *the development of the history of . . .* means simply, *the history of . . . .* Further examples:

> *We thus consider, as an atomic model, a three-level system.*
> *(We consider a three-level atomic model.)*
> *. . . requires the use of special techniques . . .*
> *(. . . requires special techniques . . .)*

In deciding whether to eliminate words, the writer must remember that few readers, if any, will search for subtle connotations, and few will necessarily assign to individual words exactly the same shade of meaning he had in mind. For instance, in the example that concerns computer programs, the main thought does not depend significantly upon the distinction between variations of the computer program and variations in the computational problems it executes. Independent of whether *variations* are assigned to *problems* or to *programs,* the point of the sentence is that programs often must be variable. Thus, although our final revision *(Many computer programs must include several variations)* did indeed suppress a possible implication (that problem variations induce program variations), few readers would have noticed this thought in either of the other versions, and its elimination is not important (in the context from which the sentence obviously came).

The point of this little analysis is that almost any revision can be said to destroy or alter some of the subtle implications in a sentence, and every writer must guard against rationalizing, on this basis, a stubborn retention of his beloved words. The ordinary reader, reading at normal speed, will not notice the subtle implications. If they are important, they should be explicitly expressed in separate sentences or at least separate clauses of their own. Otherwise, they are not important enough to retain, when the clarity of the sentence as a whole is at stake.

Hasty Phrasing

A second habit that we all acquire from speech is a proficiency in transmogrifying vagueness: The pressures of extemporaneous speech often force us to modify and qualify a vague or general word until it has been sufficiently twisted to convey our meaning. Presumably, the taboo on long silences arose because speech, with its abundant nonverbal signals, rarely requires precise words, and such apparently clumsy devices may actually be the most efficient ones in day-to-day oral communication.

But since printed words come to the reader with no emphasis or "expression" of their own, precise wording must make up the deficiency. The writer should invert his habitual techniques for finding words in speech and, instead, search at length for a precise word. In writing, modifiers should add information, not twist or limit the meaning of hastily chosen primary words. For example:

The subject of electronics . . .
(Electronics . . .)
The concept of justice . . .
(Justice . . .)
The problem of measuring X . . .)
(Measuring X . . .)
The mathematics of the theory of . . .
(The theory of . . .)
The phenomenon of snow storms . . .
(Snow storms . . .)
. . . obtain in rough proportion to effort . . .
(. . . earn . . .)
. . . show diagrammatically . . .
(. . . depict . . . or . . . display . . .)
. . . carries inevitably along with it . . .
(. . . entails . . .)
. . . intentionally leaves out of consideration . . .
(. . . ignores . . .)

. . . fail to remember . . .
  (. . . forget . . .)
extremely dark
  (black)
The question of whether . . .
  (Whether . . .)
The feature of preventing . . .
  (Preventing . . .)
. . . make it certain that . . .
  (. . . ensure . . .)
. . . has the function of providing . . .
  (. . . provides . . .)
. . . have come to occupy the place of . . .
  (. . . act as . . .)
. . . had its origin in . . .
  (. . . arose from . . .)
. . . is conducive to . . .
  (. . . favors . . . or . . . engenders . . .)
Similar in nature to that of . . .
  (Similar to . . .)
. . . such as those which . . .
  (. . . such as . . .)

Such phrases invite the reader to think first of a general concept and then immediately ask him to narrow it. In this process, he must perceive that the author intended a specific group of words to convey a single concept. Even if he notices the author's intent in passing, he may later forget whether the general or the particular was important in the original context. Admittedly, readers have had considerable practice in these mental gymnastics and may be able to execute them unconsciously, but this is no reason for a writer to require them unnecessarily.

We are not, of course, suggesting that modifiers in general be avoided. The modifier is a powerful device that can be eliminated only when its referent can be made sufficiently specific without it. We suggest, however, that before the writer starts to search for a modifier he should first search for a better noun or verb. Further, the writer should remember (from chapter III) that long qualifying phrases or strings of modifiers necessarily break up the grammatical flow, and for that reason, may even fail in their presumed purpose of careful definition: some readers may negligently skim the long phrases in an effort to recapture the grammatical sense.

Overzealousness can also produce imprecise or awkward wording. A writer may be so anxious to record the current thought before losing another lurking in the back of his mind that he hurries on without searching for precise, explicit words. Some writers may find it congenial to produce a first draft in this manner, but they should resign themselves to extensive later revision.

We suggest that a much more efficient technique in such cases is to abandon grammatical, literate writing entirely and shift to detailed outlining, which can proceed even more rapidly and is less annoying to recast properly at a later time. (Chapter VI discusses this matter more fully.)

For example, it is hard to imagine a literate writer setting down the following sentence unless he were hurried in some manner: *The use of this method should more readily enable the noise figure to be determined.* At the very least, this should be untangled to some form like: *This method should determine the noise figure more readily.* Moreover, *determine* is a vague word, and *more readily* really carries a thought that refers to *this method,* whereas the grammar refers it to the verb *enable.* Depending on the context, some form similar to the following might express the thought more clearly: *This is a particularly simple method for measuring noise figures.* If this is too short, it might be combined with the next sentence: *This simple method for measuring noise figures* . . . .

Ambiguity

A closely related difficulty in clear writing, ambiguity in the specific sense of a word, probably stems in part from habits acquired under the time limits of day-to-day speech, but peculiarities of spelling also play a role. To discuss the simpler case first, consider the letters of *object.* They spell two words, a verb and a noun, which are distinguished in speech by pronunciation, but which are identical in print ("homographs"). Again, *appropriate* represents two words, usually distinguished in pronunciation, each of which in turn has two meanings (adjective: "uniquely correct," or merely, "suitable"; verb: "seize," or merely, "reserve [for]").

Since to rule out all ambiguous words would be to proscribe most of English, particularly its strongest words, about all the writer can do is try to use words in their primary, most basic sense, and when that is not appropriate, try to ensure that the context will make the sense absolutely clear. Merely that some desired meaning is reputable and common for a given word does not mean that a reader will immediately perceive the intended sense, unless that sense has already been strongly suggested by context.

For example, unless the reader has been forewarned

by preceding material, the noun *object* (or even *aim*) might better be replaced by *goal,* which is unquestionably a noun with a relatively unique meaning. The following sentence is an example of a particularly unfortunate contextual clue: *The magazine has but two major articles in its editorial creed.* At least half the readers would assume that *article* meant *magazine article* until they reached the final two words.

In connection with word meanings, recall that the purpose of a modern dictionary is not to freeze meanings but merely to record current usage. No two people really have precisely the same notion of what a given word may mean, and all of us have rather individualistic feelings about particular words. A modern dictionary helps us to appreciate what the "average reader" is likely to understand a word to mean. It is also sometimes helpful in reminding us of common meanings that we may tend to ignore, because of our profession or background. Some writers also find a thesaurus or a dictionary of synonyms helpful, but this seems to be a matter of personal taste. No writer, however, can choose words properly without occasional reference to a dictionary.

Little words, such as prepositions, often require particular care and thought. One of the earlier sentences in this book was first set down in the form, *Printed words come before the reader* . . . . The danger that *come before* would be read as *precede* made us change this to, *Printed words come to the reader* . . . . Again, consider the phrase *constraints of orbital motion.* Except from context, there is no way to determine whether this means *constraints on* . . . or *constraints from (due to)* . . . . Even in a strong context, one of the latter forms would read more smoothly.

Similar confusions for the reader arise when the writer's intended sense obviously clashes with the grammar. For example: *The source of this discrepancy is not yet explained.* Clearly the author meant that the *discrepancy* is not yet explained. A *source* would be *discovered.* Whether such near-solecisms arise from hasty composition or purblind revision, they inevitably either delay the reader or leave him with only a vague impression of the writer's meaning.

Ordinary words deserve as much care and respect as technical terms. The proper distinctions between *force, energy,* and *power* are no more vital to clarity than, for example, the distinctions between *produce* and *induce,* between *involve* and *entail,* or between *appropriate* and *expedient.* Misuse of ordinary words betrays as much carelessness or ignorance as misuse of technical terms, and can lead to at least as much vagueness and confusion.

In particular, the writer should guard against monotonous, unintentional repetition of a word, especially in slightly different senses. This error probably occurs most commonly because the first use of a word causes it to linger in the writer's mind and to be repeated unconsciously when its approximate meaning recurs in the thought. Repetition should always be conscious and intentional, for the reader will note it and assume that it was used to emphasize recurrence of *exactly* the same concept.

Ambiguity of meaning can take so many forms that no discussion can approach completeness, and any set of examples will be more illustrative than typical. Unfortunately, the writer inherently finds particular difficulty in discovering ambiguities in his own writing, since he knows what he was trying to say. He should occasionally make conscious effort to misread his work, and in rereading, he should examine with care and suspicion any word or phrase to which he finds himself glancing back.

EMPHASIS

In the foregoing we have considered primarily faulty choice of words. The next few topics concern the proper use of words.

An attempt to be too emphatic may fail when it involves trying to strengthen an already strong word with a strong modifier. In speech, such a phrase, uttered slowly with strong emphasis on each word, may produce some effect, but even then, a single word delivered with great emphasis and followed by a pause will usually have greater effect. In writing, a series of strong words may leave the reader wondering just which one was supposed to be the most important, and much of the effect can be lost. For example, *We genuinely know the risks* and *All theories without exception share* . . . are each less emphatic than the simpler forms, *We know the risks,* or *All theories share* . . . .

Similarly, a precise word is not necessarily made more precise by modification. *Especially unique* does not mean more than *unique,* and *equally as good as* or *precisely accurate* are merely longer (and hence less emphatic) ways of saying *as good as* (or *equal to)* and *accurate* (or *precise).* The construction, *those X's which* . . . is seldom more effective than *the X's that* . . . .

A limited emphasis is available from word position. The most emphatic word of a sentence occurs at the end. The beginning of a sentence is the next most emphatic position. A short sentence is emphatic. (Each of these sentences is an example of the principle that it states.) Yet these devices lose their effectiveness if they are overworked, just as a speaker who shouted *every* word would achieve no more emphasis than he would from a quiet monotone.

Italic type is also a conventional signal for emphasis, but experience has shown that it must be used more sparingly than any other device. A reader quickly becomes accustomed to ignoring it. (It is, in fact, somewhat less clear than ordinary roman type.) If it is used sparingly, however, it will provide an unmistakable emphasis.

Finally, emphasis can be achieved by repetition. Redundancy is occasionally the secret of clear writing. (Example: these last two sentences.) Needless to say, even the pointed repetition of one particular word from sentence to sentence should be used sparingly and only when the reader will appreciate the intent. Of course, repeated use of a word that is natural to the topic of discussion will not strike the reader as emphatic. Thus the word *animal* would necessarily recur frequently in a book about zoos.

Repetition of entire thoughts in successive sentences should, of course, be reserved for thoughts of utmost importance. Repeated statement, however, is almost the only effective way to emphasize an entire thought, and it has the further advantage that the different wordings will guard against any one form being misunderstood. For this reason, the successive statements should employ varied forms and varied vocabulary. Three forms are about as many as any assertion can bear. The effect will be strongest if the most succinct (though perhaps the least precise) statement is placed last.

ALLUSION AND CONFUSION

Hinting at or alluding to ideas, the opposite of emphasis, is seldom advisable in expository writing. No reader will examine every word for hidden meanings or suggestions, and the writer should not try to insert any important suggestions with an unusual word or phrase. Most readers will skim right over it, and most of those who pause will do so because they are confused. If a sentence seems to need an extra word or phrase to suggest an idea, it should probably be scrapped and replaced by a paragraph. If the writer wishes to suggest something, he should suggest it explicitly and at sufficient length to ensure the reader's noticing it.

Elegance is neither decorative nor excusable unless it eases communication. Similarly, figures of speech, humor, and general cleverness are inappropriate unless they help to convey the message. Since they necessarily display the writer's talents and versatility, he must try to be especially honest with himself when assessing their value. Even at their best, they are somewhat distracting, and at their worst, they are exasperating because the reader must try to find the message in the midst of all the irrelevant words. If a writer has something significant to say and manages to say it clearly, the reader will be more than content.

Generalities should be kept in perspective. While everyone finds a significant new generalization interesting and appreciates having relations pointed out, the writer should beware of marginal or unnecessary generalizations. A paper on specific experiments or a special study is not an appropriate medium in which to crusade for a personal philosophy (however valid it may be). Each piece of writing should have a unified purpose, and its assertions should be confined to that purpose. Extraneous thoughts, inherently distracting to the reader, are necessarily too incomplete to impress him. Short, nagging phrases *(As always in science . . . ; Like all theoretical models . . .)* are perhaps the most annoying, since they may be attached to otherwise significant statements.

The subjunctive (conditional) form is a grammatical device that will often avert confusion, particularly in scientific writing. The subjunctive mood immediately signals to the reader that an hypothesis is recognized by the writer as untrue (or unlikely), thereby forestalling misunderstanding at the outset. For example, the form, *If there were an atmosphere on the moon,* . . . leaves no doubt in the reader's mind that the writer regards a lunar atmosphere as unlikely. By contrast, the form, *If there is an atmosphere on the moon,* . . . may leave the reader wondering what direction the argument is taking.

ABBREVIATION

We consider, finally, a few concrete topics that influence the clarity of writing.

Abbreviations are of no help to the reader. Even standard abbreviations are no simpler to read than the words they replace, for a reader can scan several complete words in less time than it takes him to recognize an abbreviation. The only justifiable reasons for abbreviating are to save writing or to save space, and neither is appropriate in plain text that is intended to convey ideas in ordinary English.

Abbreviations for physical units (cm, sec, km, . . .) form a special class. They certainly should be used in equations and tables whenever the units are at all complex, and in all but the most elementary or popular writing, such abbreviations can safely be used in every equation and with all numbers. When a unit must be mentioned in plain text, the simple, one-word names should probably be spelled out, but the more complicated ones may be abbreviated. These quantities "read" more like algebra than English to a professional. Similar exceptions, such as chemical symbols, stellar designations, legal citations, and the like, arise in other contexts. Current, skillful, professional usage is the best guide. Perhaps the next best guide is, "When in doubt, spell out."

Even previously standard Latin abbreviations should usually be suppressed. A surprising number of readers do not understand the proper distinction between *i.e.* and *e.g.* The equivalent English phrases (*that is* and *for example,* respectively) can be read so rapidly that the Latin survivals have no real value. Although *etc.* is universally understood and occasionally even used in speech, it cannot be read significantly more rapidly than *and the like,* which is actually closer to the modern meaning of *etc.* than the Latin *et cetera* itself. Certainly *etc.* should be abandoned when the intended meaning is *or the like.*

Contractions are also a form of abbreviation. Their only legitimate purpose in writing is for accurate rendering of slurred speech.

A long descriptive phrase must sometimes be used repeatedly in a discussion. To the careful writer, only two sensible courses are available, and neither of them involves coining an abbreviation. Under the first choice, the phrase must be recopied in full every time (or nearly every time) it occurs. The consequent boredom of the writer is somewhat relieved by his certain knowledge that the reader will scan and understand the full phrase faster than an abbreviation. The second alternative is to devote a short paragraph to defining and explaining a special term that will be used. Before this is done, considerable thought should be given to this special term. To be easily read, it should be a short English word or phrase; to be easily remembered, it should reflect the idea or concept that it represents; and to avoid misunderstanding, it should be sufficiently rare in such contexts to stand out clearly as a special term. In practice, such special terms are seldom really necessary in works of less than book length.

The words *latter, former* and such phrases as *the first reason, the second point* (when referring to previous material) are essentially abbreviations. Almost every reader must glance back to check their meaning. Many readers do not bother to check, hoping that the immediate context will indicate which point was meant. It appears that the human memory can retain thoughts more readily than their order of presentation. If the thoughts (*points, reasons*) have been displayed, perhaps in a numbered, indented list, then the reader can easily glance back, although he will lose some time and be somewhat distracted in doing so. In general, then, references to previous thoughts should not take these "abbreviated" forms whenever they can be avoided. Often a short phrase summarizing the earlier thought (*the practical reason, the point concerning X*) will suggest the reference quite reliably and almost as briefly.

Pronouns are also a form of abbreviation, but are

so familiar to the reader that they give him no trouble when they are properly used. About the only significant danger to a literate writer is a pronoun's attractive brevity, which may tempt him to use it in marginal cases where the antecedent, although unique, is not immediately clear. In deciding whether to use a pronoun, remember that a reader can scan three or four words in less time than the writer can set down *it*. The most frequent ineptitude is allowing an idiomatic use of *it* to intervene between the antecedent and a later pronominal *it*. For example, *If the reader loses the antecedent, it may take him some time to find it.* Here the first *it* is part of a proper idiom, but its intervention confuses the sense of the final *it*. The same effect can occur between separate sentences when a pronoun is carried along from sentence to sentence.

Colloquialisms should be avoided, not merely because they are inelegant or undignified, but because they are usually short-lived and always vague. Derogatory colloquialisms, for example, express strong but generalized disapproval, not a specific or reasoned disapproval. They might be called emotional abbreviations. Moreover, the connotations, and even the meanings, of colloquialisms vary with the age group, the geographic region, the profession, and the year.

Specialist jargon is, at best, but one small step above colloquialisms. It may seem politic to adopt the "private code" of a special field when writing something germane to it, but plain English (or at least standard technical terminology) will reach a wider audience. If one has something new or significant to say, clear words will not alienate even the specialist reader.

(Proper technical terminology supplies a precision that is truly not available in ordinary English. Jargon is either illusory precision, perhaps deceiving the writer, or a mere badge of membership.)

SPECIAL WARNINGS

Do not coin words or adopt the clumsy, redundant coinages of others. A manufactured word slows the reader while he decides upon its probable meaning, and a redundant phrase merely wastes his time. Currently popular examples are:

experimental-type	*(experimental)*
theory-wise	*(theoretically)*
continue on	*(continue)*
optimistical	*(optimistic)*
equally as good as	*(as good as)*
competency	*(competence)*
orientated	*(oriented)*
fixate	*(fix)*
argumentation	*(argument, arguing)*
systematical	*(systematic)*

and their analogs.

That and *Which:* Strictly speaking, *that* is better to introduce a defining or restrictive clause, and *which* better for a nonrestrictive, dispensable clause. Examples: *That* introduces clauses THAT cannot be omitted without destroying the meaning of the main clause. *Which* introduces parenthetic information, WHICH could be omitted without destroying the main thought.

(Note that we said that the *information* could be omitted, not necessarily the clause as it stands. This was to take into account such examples as, (*My father, who never missed his train, was annoyed with those who did.*) and (*The book, which other-*

*wise covered the subject adequately, did not anywhere de-
fine it.).* Both of the subordinate clauses are nonrestrictive
("dispensable"), even though their omission would require
changes in the main clauses as well.)

Admittedly this distinction between *that* and *which*
is not always observed, partly because an initial preposition requires *which* as object, and the distinction
must then be abandoned. Nevertheless, when it is
applicable, the distinction is surprisingly helpful, even
to readers who are unaware of it. Similarly:

While means *simultaneously with* and should be
used figuratively (adversatively) only when *simultaneously with* would serve as well.

When means *at the time of.*

Where means *at the place of.*

Finally, in closing this chapter, as in closing the
previous one, we must confess that, because the ways
of writing unclearly are almost as numerous as the
ways of writing clearly, our semisystematic discussion
cannot possibly forestall all ineptitudes, and a writer
seeking guidance must often fall back on the principles
behind our suggestions. In brief, these are:

Be explicit in at least three senses:

— Be definite, concrete, no more general than the
    context.
— Be unambiguous, unequivocal.
— Do not abbreviate, suggest, or hint.

Take time to find precise words; do not use modifiers
to twist or limit hastily chosen words with tangential
or too general meanings.

Do not invoke unnecessary generalizations; stick to
the point.

V

REACHING THE READER

THE READER'S POSITION

The position of the reader as a lone human individual attempting to apprehend the writer's message has been the basis of much that has been said on preceding pages. The reader's capacities and limitations as a fellow human being cannot fail to be apparent enough to a sufficiently thoughtful writer. He can understand them by sympathetic consideration of his own capacities and limitations and write accordingly if he remembers always his own greater familiarity with his subject. Or better still, he can analyze in the light of suggestions in this book the writers whom he reads, can thereby test his own capacities and limitations and try to write better than many of those whom he reads. As an interpreter of them, he can profit from both their skills and their ineptitudes.

But that each reader is an individual raises additional problems. Individuals are subject to infinite variation. No two readers will ever be found exactly alike, and the writer can expect no one reader to be an exact prototype of himself. Readers differ in their power of imagination, in their preference for either abstract thought or concrete illustration, in capacity for spatial visualization, in acquaintance with vocabulary, in appreciation of orderly structure, in ability to reason, in impatience with detail, and in innumerable

other ways. But most important of all, they will differ in readiness and capacity for understanding the
writer's subject matter.

In these days of close specialization, an expository
writer usually can expect to find only a limited number
of readers with a deep curiosity or a vested interest
in his special subject. Not all physicists, chemists,
biologists, psychologists, sociologists, or theologians are
equally interested in all aspects of physics, chemistry,
biology, psychology, sociology, or theology. Each man
has, certainly at any given stage of his life and more
or less permanently, his special interests within the
general area of his broad professional interests. He
cannot be expected to read with the same avidity a
discussion of any subject that does not lie within, or
border on, his area of special interest. Any author
whose work is not of general public interest, then, can
hope to find only a limited number of readers whose
interest in his message is so intense that they will
make any extraordinary effort to understand him.

The writer may be said to be truly at the center
of his subject. Around him lie in thought, wherever
they may be geographically, readers whose interests
are close to his own. Beyond these, in ever-widening
circles, lie other readers with gradually diminishing
interest in his subject. Diagrammatically, the writer
and his subject may thus be represented as at the
center of innumerable, practically infinite, concentric
circles, the area of each of which represents the range
of interests of each of his potential individual readers.
The author's purpose may then be said to be to cut a
diameter from his position at the center of his subject

across as many surrounding concentric circles as suits his purpose. Other writers will of course be at the center of other concentric circles, some perhaps close to him and others very remote. But his concern is only in spreading, as widely as he thinks desirable and possible, the influence from his center.

He should write in such a way as to accomplish this purpose. His plan, his illustrations, his vocabulary, the structure of his sentences, his definitions of terms, the pace at which his exposition moves — all the strategy of his tactical presentation — should be shaped to that end.

Any highly trained person, after struggling for many years with assigned reading, is in some danger of subconsciously assuming that every reader has a duty, an obligation, to struggle with written material until he has mastered it. But this, of course, is not at all true of mature readers. They are under no obligation to the writer. On the contrary, today's reader is overwhelmed by multitudes of writers, offering him far more material than he could ever hope to read with any care. He must inevitably pick and choose from this surfeit of riches, and he will necessarily choose only whatever he can find that stimulates him or is clearly pertinent to his work.

Only a century after printing had been developed, Sir Francis Bacon remarked wisely: "Some books are to be tasted, others to be swallowed, and some few to be chewed and digested; that is, some books are to be read only in parts; others to be read, but not curiously [carefully]; and some few to be read wholly, and with diligence and attention." Bacon classified books, but surely he would have recognized that all books are not the same to all men, that here too one man's meat may be another man's aversion. He would readily have admitted that the book one man was content to "taste" another would have eagerly "chewed and digested," have "read wholly, and with diligence and attention."

The writer's aim, then, is to be read as widely as is consistent with his purpose. But however closely he may choose to narrow his circle of influence, however few the readers he seeks, he should expect to have his work tasted by many more readers than will swallow it, and swallowed (perhaps with a grain of salt) by many more than will chew and digest it. If this was true in Bacon's time, it is true a hundredfold today, when no reader can hope to chew and digest more than a small part of the writing in the field closest to his heart. Most modern readers taste promiscuously, and when tempted to do more, swallow rapidly. Only a few cherished morsels do they find time to chew and digest, "to read wholly, and with diligence and attention." A diligent and attentive reader may have the patience and perseverance to carve the meat from chaotic heaps of fatty phrases, but the point to remember is that unless a reader has preconceived expectations of a work, he rarely approaches it with diligence and attention. He will first be a taster, and only if he likes the taste, will he consent to swallow. Few indeed will be those who chew and digest.

The writer may feel inclined to treat the taster with contempt. It is generally a mistake to do so. Among the tasters may be scholars eminent in the general field of the writer's subject but with only superficial knowledge of the limited area the writer is exclusively concerned with. The writer may at times choose to limit his communication to the intimate intellectual circle whose interests lie very close to his subject. Then he will write accordingly. But generally he will desire to extend his message at least to all readers who might have peripherally some professional interest in what he is writing about. His tasters are likely to be so much more numerous than his diligent readers, who themselves will frequently approach his work as tasters, that he will achieve his purpose best by attracting them. Even captive audiences cannot be intellectually enslaved. Nothing but the attractiveness of the subject prevents their turning their attention to something else.

All this most emphatically does not mean that the expository writer should attempt to be a mere entertainer, that he should imitate television commercials and play tricks for his reader. A taster becomes a diligent and attentive reader, or even a swallower, only when he senses sustenance in his sampling, and persists only with enrichment of the sustenance. He must be satisfied, and an intelligent, diligent reader who is not from the first approach captivated by the subject can be satisfied only with nourishing food carefully prepared and served — with firm, searching thought logically, thoroughly, explicitly, and clearly presented.

The Reader's Understanding

At this point it becomes expedient to consider somewhat more carefully the content of the concentric reader circles centered on the writer's work. It has been said that the area of each of these circles represents the potential interest of an individual reader in the writer's subject. Of what does this interest consist? Obviously of the degree of that individual reader's previous acquaintance with the writer's subject, or with allied subjects. Cardinal Newman in his most intelligent *Idea of a University* belabors the points that "Knowledge then is the indispensable condition of expansion of mind, and the instrument of attaining to it," but that "There is no enlargement [of the mind, no true learning], unless there be a comparison of ideas one with another, as they come before the mind, and a systematizing of them. We feel our minds to be growing and expanding *then,* when we not only learn, but refer what we learn to what we know already."

What the reader already knows about matters allied to the writer's subject determines whether the writer can reach him at all, and if he is to be reached, he must be met on his own ground; contact must be established with what the reader already knows. Here our analogy of the concentric circles of reader interest with the writer cutting a diameter from the center through successive circles may prove misleading. It should be borne in mind that the expanding circles of reader interest do not represent expanded interest in the writer's subject, but rather a diffusion of interest, like a gas that loses density with increased volume, so that with expanded area the circles represent diminishing interest in the subject.

Since the reader's capacity for acquiring new knowledge is restricted by what he already knows, it behooves the writer to give careful consideration to determining what readers he is addressing. If he is deliberately confining his writing to an intimate group of fellow specialists, he can assume in them a great deal of previously acquired knowledge of his subject. But if he wishes to inform a wider circle, he must at every stage of his writing bear scrupulously in mind the exact degree of their non-specialism — must determine the length of his diameter, how far into the realm of the uninformed he wishes to reach.

THE WRITER'S RESPONSIBILITY

From the two interrelated considerations set forth above (1. the elusiveness of reader interest and 2. the necessity for contact with the reader's previously acquired knowledge), certain aspects of the writer's responsibility call for evaluation or re-evaluation.

A reader is normally attracted to a piece of expository writing by its title or preliminary abstract, by the recommendation of another reader, or by his own search for something in which he is interested. He is looking for something, and he begins by sampling. He will look at the abstract, if any, at the early paragraphs, and perhaps at those just beyond obvious preliminaries, to find out more precisely what the subject is. He may read the final paragraphs to learn what conclusions have been reached, or he may simply read a bit anywhere to get the flavor of the work. He is at first a taster. As might be true of a reader of imaginative or literary writing, he will not be lured simply by beautiful prose. He is looking for facts and ideas, is asking himself, "What is the proposition? What does it signify?"

Only if he finds facts and ideas that are of interest to him will he become a serious reader. That he does not find them may not be the writer's fault. Perhaps he is not a reader for whom the work was intended. It may lie outside the range of his interests, or he may not have the requisite store of information for altogether comprehending it. The writer is at fault only if he loses readers he aimed to attract. This he may do by ineffective presentation of his material. What the reader was looking for may be concealed by poor planning or ineffective phrasing, so that a preliminary scanning does not reveal it. The writer's aim is to catch the attention of all tasters whose interests and accumulated information should place them among his serious readers. All that he can do, beyond assuring the cogency of his facts, the depth of his concepts, and the soundness of his reasoning, is to present these clearly, as for an attentive reader. Whether the taster becomes such a reader or a mere swallower will depend largely upon the effectiveness of this presentation.

Therefore the writer should make sure that the prospective reader can quickly learn what the paper is all about. If he really knew, he might want to read it; if he cannot readily find out, he may lose interest. For this reason, it is not always wise to start a paper with a purely historical summary of background material. While such material may indeed be vital for understanding the paper, and while it is especially necessary for the reader with only peripheral interests, it does not immediately tell him what he is most anxious to learn, what the paper itself has to say. It is better, when possible, to explain first the intent of the paper, as accurately as it can be stated without referring to background knowledge, then to introduce historical and background material as a continuous aid — not a preliminary — to successively more precise statements of the central proposition and its general significance.

But the writer should not rest content with introductory explanations. As the paper proceeds, he should keep the central theme constantly in the reader's mind by continual reminders of where each bit of evidence, argument, or methodology fits into the whole. The paper should have a well-defined single main purpose, and all that is written should not only serve that purpose, but also indicate clearly how it serves. Another way of phrasing essentially the same statement is, "Keep details in perspective." Never should minor issues occupy the center of the stage. They should never be allowed beyond the wings, to ensure that the reader recognizes their minor roles. The center of the stage should always be occupied by the main theme. Then any facet of the work, wherever the scanning reader's eye may light, will at least suggest the purpose of the whole.

Occasionally a mass of detail is truly unavoidable, if only to forestall possible future objections from fellow specialists. At least two devices are available to prevent such side issues from misleading or overwhelming the more casual readers. A formal appendix can sweep all such material completely out of sight. If this solution seems inelegant, an explicit announcement can forestall misunderstanding and indicate how much detail the general reader can safely skip. An equally explicit declaration when the main exposition resumes ("We now return . . .") will assure him that he has skipped to the proper place.

Finally, the paper should close with an abstract, a *precis*, or some reminder of the road that has been covered. While a list of conclusions may sometimes suffice, other forms are often better. The author must certainly hope that his readers will carry away some particular impressions. Here, at the end of the work, after all the ground has been covered and the background has been filled in, lies the perfect opportunity to explain succinctly just what impressions were intended — to etch in the reader's mind the essentials of the message and its significance.

We have urged that the reader be kept aware of both the main theme and its "significance." Although the over-all significance of a work will be decided only by its future influence, the essential point is that important implications, obvious to a specialist, will often elude a reader whose interests merely border those of the specialist. Although an author cannot foresee all possible influences of his thoughts, he should at least suggest the major, more obvious implications of his thesis, to aid the average reader in placing the message against the background of his own knowledge. By "significance" we mean the associations and ramifications that the main thesis should call to the minds of readers. "What does it mean? Why should I be interested?" These questions deserve at least suggested answers. If the reader's interest is to be aroused and maintained, he must not only perceive the message; he must also understand its significance, and if he is not a specialist in the subject, he may well require help in doing so.

Understanding, of course, is essentially a linking of new thoughts to old, the formation of connections between past knowledge and new information. The larger the number of links that are perceived, the deeper the understanding. Occasionally the new links may be so numerous as to constitute an entirely new organization of some small area of knowledge. No author can foresee all the links that others may discover between his thoughts and their own prior knowledge, but the more links he can supply without straying from his theme, the better the chance that the value of his work will be fully understood.

Probably the simplest rule in helping the reader to associate the message with his own knowledge is, "Do not force the reader to supply links that you can supply." The specialist writer may find it tedious to spell out examples and applications, but a specific illustration may be precisely what is needed to unfold for the peripherally interested reader the full significance and scope of the writer's thesis. A general rule is of little value to the reader who does not appreciate what is being generalized. "Help the Reader," for example, summarizes virtually all the principles of good writing, but those three words are of little value to one who has not examined their prolific implications.

IDEALS IN EXPOSITORY WRITING

Since, beyond the simple impact of his facts and ideas, all an expository writer can do to attract readers and gain their full attention is to present his facts and ideas effectively, some general consideration of ideals in expository writing may well close this chapter.

UNITY

Writing, even expository writing, is an art, and basic to all the arts are the interrelated principles of unity and coherence, selection and judicious arrangement of harmonious parts to produce a symmetrical whole. Samuel Taylor Coleridge, in his definition of poetry in *Biographia Literaria*, remarked: "The poet, described in ideal perfection . . . diffuses a tone and spirit of unity, that blends, and (as it were) fuses," part into part. The principle is equally significant in painting and music. The composition of both is but a blending of parts into a harmonious whole. Emerson called Greek architecture "a blended geometry," and this building art is often utilized to emphasize by analogy the compositional nature of other arts, especially writing. One is reminded of Browning's poem *Abt Vogler*, which represents the musical extemporizing of this organist as the rearing of a temple that lasts only as long as the music lasts. Artists are builders, often of things not made with hands, and no principle of their craft is more vitally imperative than the unity of their composition.

Little as the expository writer may aspire to be an artist, unity and coherence are essential in his work too. Indeed, the principles are essential to all writing, and are essential to all construction. To write at all is to construct something not made with hands, but shaped in the mind. The most superb unity may belong to the arts — if not to Deity, as Plato taught — and reach its highest literary perfection in imaginative writing. But any construction requires design, even construction of the most utilitarian of tools, machines, and household appliances.

Unity, then, is a relative quality, varying between the two extremes of perfect symmetry and the avoidance of obviously irrelevant intrusions. The highest reaches of architectural design may not be requisite for the expository writer, but he is creating something, and his composition should have architectural design. As in all utilitarian construction, his design should be a functional one. Parts should have rigorous relation to the purpose of the whole and be so arranged as to be in proper relation to each other and round out the whole. Each piece of writing presents its own individual problem. The writer should wrestle with it, for appropriate form in his discourse is of immeasurable value in attracting and satisfying readers. He need have no fear of achieving a unity too perfect for his purpose, for the unifying principle is a property of all things, from the humblest to the most exalted. Some suggestions for its achievement in expository writing will be presented in the next chapter.

PACE

Closely related to over-all design in writing is its pace. The pace of writing is essentially the spacing of its ideas, determining the speed at which it moves. Pace should be controlled at all levels, from individual sentences through paragraphs to the work as a whole. At the sentence level, thoughts can be closely packed or spaced out by expanding the grammatical forms, especially the modifiers, which may be single words, short phrases, or full clauses. At the paragraph level, the length or complexity of the sentences can be adjusted, and the number of new ideas, the span of the paragraph, will strongly affect its apparent speed of movement. The pace of the work as a whole is largely determined by the appropriate contraction or expansion of its sections.

The principle of emphasis, of course, requires that equal attention be called to parts that are of equal significance to the whole. Thus expansion of one part may call for expansion of other parts and seriously affect the length of the whole work. A writer bores his reader, to say nothing of enraging his publisher, by becoming long-winded. On the other hand, he may puzzle or confuse his reader by too much compression, by not taking the time and space to form the necessary associations between his new facts or ideas and the reader's own information concerning the subject. Here especially he must consider what sort of readers he is addressing and proceed at a pace that they can follow, but without inappropriate elaboration or detail. They do not wish to creep through his work. Nor should his excessive speed leave them breathless. He should walk side by side with his readers, accommodating his pace to his assumption of theirs, and helping them over the rough places.

Achieving the best compromise between conciseness and verbosity may require some experimentation, but it should be immediately obvious that neither extreme is desirable. If the author takes too long to say something, the reader's mind may wander; his successive associations may stray too far from the author's train of thought. But if the author machine-guns him with several important facts or ideas in sentence after sentence, the reader's mind may be riddled into insensibility while his eyes read on; he does not have time to associate the author's thoughts with his own knowledge. Brevity can be intellectually stultifying. In rare instances, this consideration may even justify slowing the pace with a temporizing phrase or doubtfully necessary information (but not in a grammatically dominant construction). In general, of course, the proper pace varies with the intended audience (and for that matter, with the quality of the writing), but it remains true that even a lay reader can be bored or lost by too slow a pace, and that even the narrowest specialist can miss important points that are hung on a single word or phrase.

A significant aspect of proper pacing is a smooth introduction. It is important to prepare the reader's mind for the subject at hand by evoking associations that will set the stage for the entrance of the message to follow. In a sense, this is a necessary phase of explaining what the paper is about, and such stage-setting should be intertwined with that explanation, not precede it. The dilemma of trying to achieve two goals at once can be ameliorated by first stating the purpose of the work in simple, general terms, and then particularizing it more and more as the background is filled in. The reader is consciously looking for an explanation of purpose, not a long preparatory discourse, and the writer should quickly satisfy the conscious need, while more subtly inserting information to satisfy the less conscious ones.

SENTENCE STRUCTURE

Related to both design and pace is sentence structure. Unity, as has been said, is a universal principle, and each sentence has its own design, which must be grammatical to be intelligible, but can be grammatical without being at all intelligible. Sentences may also be conceived of as the paces in pacing. They determine the rate of movement, and each must be effective if movement is not to be impeded. The test of a sentence is what it accomplishes and whether it accomplishes its proper function in its place. As the expression of a single complete thought, it is the unit of accomplishment in writing, a "mindful" of thought. Sentences should therefore be functional, and every word in them should be functional. Like the whole work of which they are parts, and for the sake of that satisfying whole, they should be neither over-expanded nor over-concentrated, but always adequate to express thoroughly and clearly the thought they were designed to bear, with no useless words lingering in them anywhere. Details of sentence structure are considered in chapters VII and VIII of Part II.

VOCABULARY

As sentences are simply words, properly chosen, arranged, and punctuated, vocabulary becomes the ultimate unit of effective communication. For the technical writer, vocabulary is also an important aspect of pace, for he can proceed more rapidly by writing directly in technical terms, but he then outruns any reader not familiar with those terms. He is faced with a dilemma. For if he takes up too much of his fellow specialists' time to explain terms familiar to them, he may exasperate them, and if he does not explain technical terms, he may puzzle or fail to reach uninformed readers.

Here again he must decide the extent of the audience he seeks. If he seeks readers outside his own narrow circle, he must either explain or avoid some technical terms. Specialists are human too, despite some opinions to the contrary, and even those closest to his circle are perhaps less desirous than he thinks to have thoughts couched in their own narrow jargon. His reputation depends more upon his thoughts than his vocabulary, and even the technically informed may well feel satisfaction at finding abstruse thought expressed in plain English. The best way out of the dilemma is probably to use language as popular as is consistent with both one's purpose in reaching readers and with precision of meaning, and then, in work not addressed to close specialist groups, to define essential technical terms. Even though definition may slow the pace, intelligibility is always more to be desired than speed.

DEGREE OF OBJECTIVITY

Another dilemma in expository writing lies in selecting the proper degree of objectivity. Even in scientific writing, objectivity can be overdone. Science and other types of knowledge progress, not through any lack of various personal prejudices, but through their mutual cancellation and rectification as the evidence accumulates. "Scientific objectivity" is not a coldness toward ideas, but merely a willingness to tell the whole truth with utmost conscientiousness. In reality, no serious author writes about ideas that he finds uninteresting, and the reader knows this as well as the author does.

The implications of these homilies for the writer are that comments upon evidence or ideas should not be suppressed. If a hypothesis is unconventional, if a temperature is surprisingly high or a resonance unusually narrow, this qualitative fact should be pointed out by inserting at least an adjective or an adverb into the sentence that states the quantitative fact. Although a specialist might notice the unusual size of a number or the strange turn of an argument, the peripherally interested reader will not. Let the reader see what the facts and ideas mean. Facts do not "speak for themselves" to non-specialists as they do to specialists, and if the specialist may be expected to notice something unusual, the non-specialist should certainly be allowed to reorient his thinking in the same manner. These little aids to peripherally interested readers require only a few extra comment-words here and there, and omitting them is merely a false show of objectivity, or worse, an annoying display of the author's erudition.

Yet the opposite extreme, of course, is equally to be avoided. In most expository writing, the author is not recounting his personal experiences, but is explaining thoughts or observations that should be accepted or rejected on the basis of their own validity. The reader's attention should therefore be directed toward the message and its validity, not toward the author's personal feelings about it. Although helpful comments and qualitative remarks should not be suppressed, the asides should not become so numerous, nor range so far, as to shift the reader's attention away from the message and toward the author as a person. The writer should maintain sufficient professional dignity to avoid placing himself at the center of the stage. He should try to be an efficient master of ceremonies, but not the featured attraction.

Even temporary indulgence in the temptation to make a show of one's self can be harmful in another way. The personal display of "purple prose" is not only a practice as objectionable as the excessive objectivity of "pallid prose," but patches of it will seriously mar the indispensable quality of unity. Unity, once it is established in the plan, is largely maintained by "tone," by assumption of, and persistence in, a proper mean between the extremes of the purple and the pallid. Maintenance of tone blends properly related parts into an emotionally, as well as an architecturally, symmetrical whole.

THE WRITER'S VOICE

Proper tone is not, however, merely a matter of degree of subjectivity, although subjectivity displays it. It is actually a complex amalgam of the writer's total attitude and personality, and as the word "tone" implies, it is expressed largely, though not exclusively, through sound. Clear expression of meaning is the staff of intellectual life, but few readers can be maintained in a state of animated interest by meaning alone. Although writing and speaking are quite different processes, requiring different techniques, it should never be forgotten that language is basically speech, a succession of sounds. Letters are as truly symbols of sounds as are notes on a musical scale, though they differ from notes because they symbolize much more than sound. The writer speaks to the reader, and his voice is heard by the sensitive reader, who apprehends meaning much better when it is blended with sound.

The voice of the writer is itself a blend of many elements, but most dominant in it are rhythm and alliteration. Rhythm is produced by successive waves of sound, something different from the sound waves of the physicist because much longer and slower. Good writing flows and ebbs like the waves of the ocean, and on a somewhat similar time interval. The conventional meters of poetry of course carry rhythm to its fullest extreme in language, but prose too has its rhythms. The rhythms of prose, like those of poetry, are mainly structural, but of a much longer interval and much rougher structure. They occupy an interval more akin to the poetic line, or verse, than to the poetic foot, and they have no intricate and delicately balanced subdivisions such as the feet that compose the poetic verse. Prose rhythms are created by regular, but also varying, stages of structure within a sentence or from sentence to sentence. The reader should be able to ride the writer's structural waves, with almost but not quite continuous spurts of attentiveness, separated by infinitesimal instants of relaxation. The span of the reader's attentiveness is maintained unconsciously by the experienced writer. Others must learn it by attentive reading and practice in writing.

Aside from their rhythms, the musical quality of both poetry and prose is largely alliterative. As has been said, letters are symbols of sounds, and since writing is a substitute for speech, letters should evoke sounds for the reader, and for most readers they do. The interplay of these sounds constitutes alliteration. Language cannot be divorced from sounds because it essentially is sounds. Sounds are inevitable, and the problem is to make them speak, to see that they conform to one's message and do not distract from it. This is not the place to undertake an exhaustive study of alliteration, and most such studies seem not to have helped very much, for the subject is as inexhaustible as the possible combinations of the multiplicity of sounds symbolized by the letters in our language. Any reader with ordinary human perceptiveness will sense the difference between the sounds of such phrases as "chaotic cacophony" or "bungling bombast" and Tennyson's

> The moan of doves in immemorial elms,
> And murmuring of innumerable bees.

The point is not that everyone should write like Tennyson. Any one of the three phrases might be right in its proper place, as Tennyson's was right in *The Princess*. The point is, rather, that the sound should suit the sense, re-enforcing and supporting it.

Notice that the sound-message of the above phrases is not conveyed solely by initial sounds of words. In the first phrase the harsh "k" sound occurs four times, the ominous "a" and "o" in five places. "Chaotic" ends with the startling "tic," and "cacophony" begins its final fall with the derisive "f" of "phony." In the second phrase the threatening blow of "b" occurs three times, supported first by the growl of "ungl," then the hum of "om," and finally the hiss of "ast," to contrast with the alarm bell of "ling." We will leave the liquid melody of Tennyson's subtle interweaving of "m's," "n's," "l's," "r's," and "s's," his vowel variations, and interspersed "d's" and "v's," with the terminal "bees," for the reader's analysis.

Of such interlaced sounds is our language composed. It is all sound, and despite some contrary opinions, the sound of no individual letter is in itself objectionable. Nor is alliteration in itself either good or bad. It is simply unavoidable. Its proper use cannot be reduced to a rule, or rules. As Alexander Pope remarked, "The sound must seem an echo to the sense." The writer must "play it by ear." He should listen to his own words, for the reader will hear them, and must try to assure that matched waves of sound and meaning advance his work in cadenced order, giving his voice the appropriate tone.

ANALOGY AND METAPHOR

The distinction between simple analogy and figurative metaphor (or simile) is not a strict one, but it can be drawn. Analogy compares objects, situations, or ideas that can be related logically. It attempts to clarify a less familiar concept by comparing it to a concept that is more familiar, as in the likening of variations in reader interest to concentric circles in the early part of this chapter. Its purpose is to promote clearer understanding of the less familiar, and it is so highly an intellectual device that, in a sort of pseudo-logic, "reasoning by analogy" is recognized. A truly helpful comparison of this kind is not only often permissible, but frequently throws welcome light on a foggy situation. The danger is that it may be mistaken for an inept and false "argument" by analogy. If this danger is avoided, analogy can be a powerful aid to understanding, often evoking subtle associations on a more general level than could be maintained in an example or application. Labelling an analogy with a specific announcement, or even an explicit disclaimer, will avoid any misunderstanding of its role, and a more or less continuous grammatical labelling is possible if it is cast entirely in the conditional subjunctive mood.

Metaphor (or simile) compares objects, situations, or ideas that are essentially of different classes. Much metaphor is enshrined in our language as a prominent part of our regular vocabulary ("ships *plow* the sea"; "a *volley* of oaths") and is known as "dead" metaphor because its metaphorical character is no longer recognized. "Live" metaphor (as must once have been true of all "dead" metaphor) gains much of its power from unexpected recognition of likeness that startles and pleases largely because of its originality. Metaphor, like analogy, aims to clarify by comparison of the less familiar to the more familiar, but as is not always true of the more pedestrian analogy, its comparisons are to the highly concrete. It attempts to make the abstract or less concrete more concrete. It therefore evokes images, appeals strongly to the senses and the emotions, invites the reader to see, hear, taste, smell, or touch. Being vividly sensory and emotional, it is less intellectual than simple analogy and threatens less danger of being confused with presentation of false evidence, though a similar danger may threaten in the substitution of its dazzling brilliance for the steadier light of understanding.

Metaphor, at least "dead" metaphor, cannot be avoided by any user of the language, and since, as was remarked at the beginning of this chapter, all readers are human, and sense and emotional experience are such revealing and pleasing aspects of human life, fresh or "live" metaphor should not be shunned either. The danger, as remarked above, is that its vividness may distract the reader. By its very nature, it flashes into the reader's mind a concept basically different from that of the context, and may substitute for it, enticing the reader, at least for the moment, down a primrose path over which his mind may wander and stray from the subject. Yet metaphors, like analogies, into which they blend,* can make a valuable contribution to prevention of too monotonous objectivity of style and brighten the way, especially for the peripherally interested reader, at the same time that they enlighten his understanding. They should always be strictly germane to the subject, never indulged in just to entertain the reader, who seeks and demands understanding, and finds them entertaining only as they deepen his understanding. Festoons of figures, common in "purple" prose, and more legitimate in imaginative writing, are distinctly not appropriate to expository writing.

----

* Consider Bacon's famous pronouncement on books cited above (p. 63). This begins as metaphor, but Bacon's literal interpretation of it transforms the metaphor into analogy, and considerable use of this analogy was made in this chapter.

INSPIRATION OF READERS

All the foregoing involves establishing contact with readers, if possible with attentive and diligent readers, in order that the writer's thoughts may enter and influence other thoughtful minds. Yet another prospect of influence remains. The effective writer may inspire the thoughtful reader to fresh thought of his own. Emerson, in his famous address *The American Scholar,* said of books, "They are for nothing but to inspire." This is a gross exaggeration, as Emerson must have realized, for he almost at once qualified it. Books inform, and even among the enticements of television, they still have a considerable reputation for entertainment. But they also inspire. "One must," as Emerson adds, "be an inventor to read well." The good writer kindles a fire among the thoughts of his reader.

This fact has been nowhere more apparent than in science, the area in which human thought has been manifestly most effective. Physics and astronomy are based largely on Newton. But Newton had illustrious predecessors — Aristotle, Ptolemy, Roger Bacon, Copernicus, Galileo, Kepler, Descartes, to mention only a few luminous stars in a great galaxy — and illustrious, but disdained, contemporaries in Leibnitz and Robert Hooke. Yet if Newton could investigate modern physics, developed through a similar chain of great thinkers who have followed his leads, he would doubtless be delighted with the penetrations and proliferations of his theories, and at the same time, from what we know of his character, perhaps chagrined that he had not carried to greater fruition the implications of his own thought. Darwin has a similar position in biology, with many influential predecessors, in-

cluding his own grandfather, and with two great contemporaries in Alfred Russel Wallace, whom he treated
much better than Newton treated Hooke, and Thomas
Henry Huxley, who applied Darwin's theory to man
before Darwin did, and with many great successors,
notably Mendel. Dalton has a similar position in
chemistry, and Freud in psychology.

These are illustrious names, or in the instances of
Hooke and Wallace names that deserve more luster
than they have acquired. But the whole great history
of science records a similar chain-reaction of thought
from mind to mind. Countless lesser luminaries than
these, and many of as great or nearly equal magnitude,
have handed on the torch of illumination and increased
its glow. Books, then, in their impacts on other minds
may open ever new channels of thought and have far-
reaching effects, far beyond their writers' conscious
intention and beyond the horizons of their writers'
understanding. A primary hope for this little book is
that it may inspire some of its readers to improve their
writing, even in ways beyond the scope of its suggestions. Indeed, this whole chapter was suggested to
us by our reading of another book on writing from
which little or nothing is used here, and to which much
asserted here is contradictory. Nevertheless, that book
inspired this chapter.

PART II

MECHANICS

VI

THE SHUFFLE DRAFT — HOW TO START

The writer has two jobs: to formulate his message, and to express it. Unlike the extemporaneous speaker, the writer need not perform these tasks simultaneously. Indeed, this would be the least efficient procedure. The only sensible, efficient method is to know what to say before trying to find an effective way of saying it. This is a truism, to be sure, but it has implications that inexperienced writers are often unwilling to grant. Perhaps the habit, unavoidable in speech, of "composing on the run" suggests that forethought and planning are not really necessary. Perhaps the act of setting down words that are not final seems intuitively inefficient.

But finding precise words and unobtrusive grammar requires too much concentration for a writer also to keep in mind his complete message and its ramifications. A careful writer soon discovers that many painfully written passages must be scrapped if detailed plans have not been laid out before starting to write in earnest. It is both frustrating and wasteful to find that carefully written material must be thrown out because, although it is crystal clear, it does not say the right things in the right sequence.

Poor or illogical organization cannot be overcome by "polishing" the manuscript or by other purely editorial work. When the order of the ideas must be changed, almost every sentence will fall into a new context and must be completely rewritten. Nor can poor organization be cured by adding "explanatory" introductions or summaries. They do not change the obscure or confusing sequence of ideas; they merely add more bulk to further discourage the reader. This is why so few company editorial offices seem able to make any startling improvements in the material they receive. Once an author has written his "rough" draft, it is already too late to cure any deep faults. Complete rewriting is then the only truly effective cure, and the author himself is the only person who can do it properly.

PRELIMINARIES

Before setting a single word on paper, then, the prospective writer should first formulate for himself specific answers to two questions:

(1) "*Who* are the readers I wish to reach?"
(2) "*What* is the thesis I wish to convey?"

He should not merely "consider" these questions; he should work out explicit, detailed answers to them. Only then can he picture the readers' backgrounds and interests; only then can he decide what he must tell them to support his message. Although a writer may occasionally solve some of these problems unconsciously as he forms a decision to write something, it is only prudent to confirm these vital preliminaries by answering these fundamental "*who* and *what*" questions explicitly.

In particular, if the readers include groups with incompatible interests, organizing the material and guiding the various sorts of readers through it will be especially difficult. Some readers may wish to see a great deal of detail and supporting evidence; others may wish to see applications and illustrations; and still others may wish to see only final conclusions or recommendations. If different papers, addressed to different groups, are not practical, the materials to meet these various needs must be combined in a way that will allow each reader to find what he most requires. Different types of material should not be interlaced, as they might be for a homogeneous set of readers, and adequate guidance will have to be provided by an initial explanation of the organization, followed by generous use of section headings, subtitles, and explicit directions.

Thus, if the writer first decides *who* his readers will be and then determines *what* he must tell them to convey his message, many broad problems of selecting and organizing material will be implicitly solved. Many more such problems will remain, but the broad principles will be brought to his attention, and the dangers of false starts or misdirected efforts will be minimized.

PLANNING

Traditional planning devices are the outline and the rough draft. As the terms are currently understood, however, these devices do not serve nearly so well as an intermediate device. For frequently an outline is a mere table of contents, a list of main topics with perhaps a few subtopics, whereas a rough draft or first draft is usually a grammatically complete paper that might be (and frequently is, alas) put into print more or less as it stands. In these senses, at least, an outline represents too little planning, and a rough draft too much ill-considered effort. The best tactic is "divide and conquer."

The most efficient device might be called a "shuffle draft." It should be less tabular in form and far more detailed than an outline, but also much less presentable than any first draft. The point is to experiment with arrangements of the complete message, with all its detailed subsequences of ideas, without any need to put these ideas into words — or at least into words that others would understand. A shuffle draft is a detailed but telegraphic, ungrammatical, entirely private rehearsal of the full work. It is a full set of detailed notes in whatever form the writer (to be) cares to scribble them.

The ideal is to complete all necessary experimentation with the thought before turning to the task of writing clear English. If the shuffle draft has been properly completed, it requires only translation into English to become the final paper, and the writer can then devote his entire attention to expressing clearly his prearranged thoughts.

Scribbling private, telegraphic notes and mnemonic phrases is so simple that the shuffle draft should never be omitted merely because it involves a little time and physical effort. Even when everything appears straightforward at the outset, a shuffle draft followed by an essentially final draft will actually consume less time than a directly composed first draft. Although it is possible to compose good written English and to think about organization at the same time, this double-headed task is slow, unnecessary, and actually inefficient for writing anything longer than a letter.

Language is one-dimensional in the sense that it can

present ideas only in linear sequence, while the human mind often seems to view relationships in a more tangled, multi-dimensional manner. Perhaps this is why intimate knowledge of a topic does not, in fact, guarantee that a writer can immediately launch into a lucid exposition of it. One of the greatest difficulties in organizing a work (aside from selecting the truly cogent thoughts) is to find the clearest way of arranging the thoughts in a linear, progressive series. In extemporaneous speech, such difficulties are unavoidable, and indeed, usually entail frequent restatements and circuitous discussion before mutual understanding is achieved. Similar difficulties arise in writing, but the writer can minimize such wasted effort by testing many serial arrangements of his thoughts before he seriously attempts to express any one series intelligibly.

Moreover, it is common experience that attempting to set down an argument or explain a complex matter to others is one of the best ways to force oneself to think out vague ideas and organize them into a coherent logical series. Similarly, the writer finds that the shuffle draft seldom ends in the form that he initially envisioned. As the thoughts are laid out serially on paper, an important insertion or a better arrangement almost always springs to mind. In the simple shuffle draft, even drastic changes of this sort are a comparatively simple matter.

The writer thereby faces his two main problems one by one. In arriving at a satisfactory shuffle draft, he organizes his message and background material into the most logical serial order. He assures himself that his arguments and illustrations are sound and properly arranged. He can eliminate unnecessary asides and adjust the balance of emphasis. In particular, there should be little danger of launching into exhaustive treatments of minor issues. He can note where parenthetic material is unavoidable, where the reader should be warned of sudden changes in point of view, and where special emphasis will be needed.

Perhaps the foregoing description has glossed over some practical complications, such as human fallibility, which may occasionally prevent an ideal separation of the tasks, but detailed planning and forethought can save considerable unnecessary labor and wasted effort, even when one is writing for a deadline. Workmanlike results in any field require planning as well as skill, and writing is no exception.

METHOD

So much for the theory and exhortations. How does one go to work? The shuffle draft is usually developed by successively refining a rough outline. Start immediately by jotting down some major topics. Writing down even a few rough headings frees the mind to think about the material that will go under these headings. Jot down notes or mnemonic phrases as items come to mind. Muddle along; do not try to get even the main headings correct at first. As more and more details spring to mind, one is almost sure to want to reorganize them, perhaps completely. This is the advantage of the technique. A page or two of scribblings can be discarded and replaced with no qualms and very little trouble. Hastily scribbled private notes that need be decodable only by the writer can be produced very rapidly and can be cut, pasted, rearranged, festooned with inserts, scrapped, and recopied with relatively little wasted time or effort.

Above all, waste no effort in being literate. Only later, after the paper has emerged in this shuffle draft, essentially complete in all its thoughts, will it be profitable to search for intelligible phrasing.

A few variants on this method of planning should be mentioned for completeness. If cogent phrases come to mind, they may, of course, be recorded amidst the otherwise more private notes. The point is not to waste time consciously searching for them.

If special terminology will be required, it should receive careful consideration at an early stage. Special concepts should be given names that are both suggestive and fairly short. If a few English words will not adequately describe the concept, try to pick a name that is both unusual and suggestive — unusual to ensure that the reader will recognize that it is a special term, and suggestive to ensure that he will remember its meaning.

If very much mathematics or a number of diagrams are involved, some scheme for cross-referencing to one's day-to-day records may help to save recopying. Sometimes, merely jotting down the first few symbols of an equation, or a few of the key symbols, will sufficiently identify it for private purposes.

In shorter works, the advantage of spreading everything out on a few large sheets usually outweighs the disadvantage of frequent recopying, but for large works (such as a small book), the material cannot all be spread out on a desk top. Then the fact that index cards can be rearranged without recopying becomes a major advantage. To exploit this advantage, write only one item (or a few very closely related items) on each card, and do not number the cards. If equation numbers or other cross-references are necessary, use a decimal numbering system to allow for insertions. Some or all cards may occasionally require recopying for a variety of reasons, but if new items are always started on new cards, recopying will not be necessary nearly as frequently as it would be with a rough manuscript. (Or, conversely, advisable rearrangements will not be neglected.) A small, loose-leaf notebook can be almost as useful if it, too, is properly used by starting each new topic on a new page to allow for later rearrangements or insertions.

> When a deck of index cards becomes large, some scheme for preserving its approximate order and for separating its main sections may be helpful. A diagonal crayon or pencil mark across the edge of the deck will indicate the general sequence (mark heavily enough to touch every card). Separate or differently colored edge marks can distinguish main sections. Tabbed "alphabetic-index-index" cards can be reversed and headings written on the backs of the tabs. If a complete reorganization destroys the value of edge marks, new heavier marks can easily be made on another part of the edges.

CHECKING THE PLANS

Whatever detailed variants are employed, the following points should be checked with particular care as the shuffle draft nears completion.

(1) The introduction should tell the reader what he can expect to gain from reading the rest of the paper. That is, it should tell him not merely where he will start but also where he will arrive and something about how he will get there. This is the surest way of motivating the reader of expository writing.

(2) Each shift in subject or method should be noted. At such points the reader should be explicitly told what change is about to occur. Similarly, any digressions should be announced beforehand and closed with an explicit statement that the main argu-

ment is to be resumed. Alternatively, the advisability of a formal appendix should be considered.

(3) Each item in the shuffle draft should generally require a paragraph or less in the final paper. Where an item appears to require more than a paragraph, the necessary details should be noted under it. In short, the plans should be completed.

(4) Where a thought requires special emphasis, the means of achieving this emphasis should be considered. A well-chosen heading or subtitle is especially effective. If repetition appears to be appropriate, jot down a number of alternate expressions, preferably with considerable variation in structure and vocabulary, to ensure that the thought will be neither missed nor misinterpreted.

(5) Denials may be as important as assertions. Be sure that the reader cannot interpret omission of a reference or a topic as an implication that it is incorrect or unimportant (unless such an implication is intended; even then, an explicit statement would be more honest). Similarly, ensure that no reader can assume the argument to be "against" a position that is merely not discussed or to which a "separate but equal" alternative is being offered. In short, forestall any unintended implications that even a hypothetical hostile reader might manage to read into the paper.

Such denials should be kept short, since readers quickly tire of being told what the writer is not saying, but a few short sentences in the interests of clarity are welcomed, even by those who do not necessarily require them.

(6) The paper should close with a backward glance over the material that has been covered. Conclusions should be summarized, and the reader should be re-

minded of the methods by which the conclusions were reached. Sometimes there may not be any strict conclusions, but the paper presumably has some point that the reader should carry away. The final paragraphs should tell him what the writer expected this to be.

Paragraph Development

Paragraph divisions are the main links between the shuffle draft and the first draft of the final work. Although the correspondence is not always perfect, an item in the shuffle draft usually corresponds to a paragraph in the final paper, and conversely paragraph divisions should show the reader how individual thoughts have been grouped to develop items in the full message.

The principles of paragraphing in expository writing are peculiar to expository (and argumentative) writing. In narration, paragraphing is by episodes, a change of incident calling for a new paragraph. In description (insofar as the extension of the description may call for paragraphing), the basis is to call attention to a new object or a different aspect of an object. But in expository writing, paragraphs identify stages of thought. The indentation signals to the eye of the reader that his mind is expected at that point to switch to a new track. The angle of deflection may be great or it may be slight, but it must be there.

Expository paragraphing, essentially a grouping of sentences, therefore relates the over-all plan of the whole work to the content of individual sentences. It groups sentences so that the group may perform its proper function in fulfilling the purpose of the whole work. The indentation that starts a paragraph is a form of punctuation, signaling a change in the general development of the thought, just as conventional punctuation signals nuances of construction and thought relation within the sentence.

Through its relation to the work as a whole, the paragraph performs for the writer a quite different function from that of the sentence. The sentence may be said to be the unit of performance, the unit of thought, embracing what the mind of either writer or reader can encompass at one time, corresponding to an armful or a handful in physical accomplishment. The paragraph, on the other hand, may be said to represent for the writer a unit of forethought, an item in the over-all plan or shuffle draft. Its content is as small a unit of his whole as the writer can foresee to be essential in expression of that whole. He can plan individual sentences only as he writes them, but he can make preliminary provision for each paragraph as a necessary part of his compositional purpose.

The length of a paragraph is determined by two somewhat conflicting requirements. The first of these is of course the unity of its content. Each paragraph should advance a distinguishably different topic, or different phase of a topic, from those of the paragraphs that precede and follow it. But each paragraph should also be adjusted to the attention span of a reader, and attention spans of modern readers seem to be shorter than the attention spans of readers once were, perhaps because of the distractions to which modern readers are frequently subjected. It is, at any rate, dangerous to extend the length of paragraphs beyond normal limits in expository writing, lest the content of the paragraph confuse the reader by compelling his attention to more ideas than he is capable of accepting as a unit. On the other hand, to paragraph too frequently is to fragmentize the content so that the reader has difficulty apprehending it all as the unit it should be. The writer should maintain, then, a normal length of paragraphs, from which he departs only occasionally and for good reason, and he must at the same time so manage his paragraphs that each clearly performs its own assigned task and only that task.

A writer will frequently find that he has extended a paragraph too far, that in zealous pursuit of his topic he has found more to say about it than he anticipated. Then a simple survey of what has been written will often reveal a place where a somewhat unconscious shift to another phase of the subject has occurred, and where with very little, and sometimes no, rewording a new paragraph may start. If no such division of the material can be found, rethinking and rewriting may be required to divide the discussion into manageable paragraph units. Too short paragraphs are, however, just as objectionable as too long ones, and the writer must take care that in avoiding the Scylla of the one he does not fall into the Charybdis of the other.

A valuable guide to the content of a paragraph for both writer and reader is the so-called "topic sentence." This is a sentence in which the general meaning of the paragraph is summed up. It may occur anywhere in the paragraph, or even in well-written paragraphs it may not occur at all. The normal position for it, however, is near the beginning of the paragraph, and in this position it serves its directive purpose best, reminds the writer and informs the reader what the paragraph is about. Sometimes such a statement at the beginning of the paragraph is not feasible. Then it can be worked around to at the end or elsewhere. Its presence somewhere in the paragraph is always helpful.

The function of the paragraph is to develop or expand a concept. That the writer has expressed his concept, even expressed it clearly, does not assure that the reader will comprehend all that it means to the writer. The writer must attempt, through development of his thought, to express, not just the thought itself, but all the relevant ramifications and significances it has for him, so that the reader may, in so far as is possible, see mind's eye to mind's eye with the writer — not only apprehend the generalization but comprehend (fully embrace) its specific details and implications. The writer thus not only pinpoints his precise position for the reader, but draws a map of the surrounding territory, opening paths of approach for varieties of readers.

The development of an expository paragraph will generally take one of three forms, or present some combination of them. Its purposes are usually to explain, to prove, or to emphasize. By "explanation" is meant full and complete elaboration, analytical dissection of an idea, insofar as is essential to full understanding of it. Restatement, instances, illustrations, and examples are often required, so that if the reader does not fully grasp the idea in one form he may in another. By "proof" is meant the evidence as to why an idea or position should be accepted, why it should be believed as well as understood. And by "emphasis" is meant assertion and demonstration of the significance of the fact or thought, how it pertains to the writer's purpose, and what position it assumes in that purpose. Other functions for paragraphs may arise, and sometimes one of these functions may be spread through a number of paragraphs, or more than one function may be telescoped into one paragraph, but in general these three functions are those of expository writing, and paragraphs are the successive steps in such writing.

Introduction, Further Suggestions

Since even experienced writers usually find the beginning of a work the most difficult part, we consider a few more detailed suggestions for organizing an introduction.

Say something significant in the first sentence. By "significant" we mean not merely true, but also new to the reader, although not necessarily startling. One good plan is, in effect, to assume that the reader has not read the title. Do not refer to it, but restate explicitly whatever thought the title was intended to suggest. Then develop this "expanded title" by showing how the message of the paper fits into the field to which it is germane and by explaining terms and concepts if necessary.

This is an excellent opportunity to bring in background material that will help as many nonspecialist readers as possible. With a little skill and imagination, the writer can initiate the nonspecialist and entertain the specialist with an apt summary of the stage setting and the significant points of contact between the present state of the field and the message of the paper.

Similar opportunities will arise later, whenever a term or concept is introduced for the first time. A nonspecialist reader may be lost if no definition is given, and a specialist will not be offended by an accurate, succinct definition (he may even be pleased to have it).

In the introduction, after setting the stage, describe briefly the approach and methods that will be used and the conclusions to which they will lead. While a slavish listing and summary of each later section is not always necessary, some guidance for the reader should be provided. In particular, if there is elementary material or the like, the reader should be told where it is, or where various readers should begin reading. The reader who may wish primarily to see a detailed statement of the conclusions (or other natural divisions of the message) should be told where to find it. In short, the purpose is to make the paper useful to as many different types of readers as is practical.

General Precautions

As regards the paper in general, the following points should be kept in mind.

Do not apologize for elementary material. Because apologies distract the reader and waste his time, their effect is largely self-cancelling. A clear statement of fundamental facts never offends anyone. If the review material is especially lengthy and there is genuine danger of losing a sophisticated reader who might be interested in still later material, state, directly and simply with no wasted words, that review material follows and extends to such and such a point.

Do not set up a straw man only to demolish him. The reader will be annoyed at being misled into following detailed arguments that only lead him back to where he started. If a current misconception must be recognized and described in some detail to make the writer's objections clear, then this parenthetic description should be labelled as such by a prior announcement, and it should be couched in conditional, subjunctive form to make the writer's position continuously clear.

We cannot emphasize too strongly the value of definitions and explanations. It requires only a sentence or two to define a term, explain mathematical notation, or summarize a concept. Composing such sentences may be a nuisance to the specialist writer, but these few sentences will often retain a reader who would otherwise lay the paper down because, although he finds it interesting, it is not "in his field."

Brevity is usually desirable, but revision may sometimes produce unduly short sentences. Often one sentence can be made a subordinate clause of a preceding or succeeding sentence. In such cases, as always, be sure that the most important thought is contained in the main clause of the resulting complex sentence. If entire sections of the paper seem too short, they should be lengthened, if at all, only by adding significant, substantive material, such as examples, illustrations, analogies, further details, and the like. Generalities or philosophical reflections usually cannot be sufficiently developed to convince, or even particularly interest, the reader.

Writing under the pressure of a deadline is unfortunately common. As in performing any other job under pressure, corners must be cut, and an incomplete performance must be made to serve. Individual judgement is the only final guide, but we suggest that neither planning nor rewriting should be eliminated. The result cannot be clear if it is not properly organized, if it jumps from subject to subject and back, or if thoughts that belong in the middle are tacked at the end. On the other hand, if a large number of well-organized ideas are presented in vague language or contorted grammar, readers may actually grasp only a random sampling of them.

In general, of course, our suggestions for expressive writing are contained in chapters III and IV, which attempted to discuss, as systematically as the nature of the problems would allow, various means for guiding the reader unobtrusively through the grammatical constructions and for expressing thoughts in forms that will be precise and explicit in print. We can add little to those discussions.

In summary, the message of this chapter is planning. Despite his contrary habits in speaking, the writer should map out his thoughts in essentially complete detail before attempting to compose clear English expression for them. To ensure that the planning is complete, the best mechanical aid is a "shuffle draft," a draft that is essentially complete but that contains only the thoughts, in the sense that the language is still private, perhaps telegraphic, and even ungrammatical. By thus dividing his work into two separate tasks, planning first and expression second, a writer can give each task in turn his undivided attention. Only after the shuffle draft has been completed and checked for adequate guidance to the reader, is it efficient to search consciously for explicit wording and unobtrusive grammar. With the shuffle draft laid out before him, the writer can devote virtually his entire attention to the major problems of expression, as discussed at length in Part I.

The next two chapters contain summaries of grammar and punctuation, to which the practicing writer must occasionally refer. The succeeding, final chapter discusses techniques for locating and polishing rough spots that remain after the writing has been essentially completed.

VII

GRAMMATICAL COMMENTARY

It was once thought, chiefly by the not-quite-expert, that every language should have an inherent, "correct" structure, and that only sentences conforming to the unchanging rules of the ideal, proper structure could be "correct." Nowadays, it is widely recognized that no grammatical construction or scheme of punctuation is, in itself, more "right" than any other.

But this does not mean that modern rules of grammar and punctuation are valueless, or that they can be ignored! The newer attitude stresses that the rules of any one age are not necessarily those of another. But no one can sanely deny that every age has its common agreements concerning what constitutes native speech or writing, as opposed to what is considered alien — the unconsciously amusing linguistic concoctions of those who do not really "know" the language.

Indeed, it could hardly be otherwise: much communication with completely unrelated, isolated words would scarcely be possible. Conventions, conscious or not, must specify the *relations between words* and *are vital to the meaning* of any series of words. If anyone doubts this, let him try scrambling the word-order in any reasonably complicated English sentence and observe what happens to its meaning. Such relations between words are the prime (if not the sole) feature that distinguishes a human language from a mere system of isolated, unrelated signals, such as many animals and even insects employ.

The task of grammar, then, is to codify the current, largely unconscious, conventions regarding the function and meaning of words — to distill these conventions into condensed statements that offer reasonably quick and fairly reliable tests for deciding whether a sentence will be undistracting, easy to read, and easy to understand. It is clear, of course, that such a task can never be truly completed. The rules will always have exceptions, because the conventions of language in any age are occasionally illogical and perhaps even contradictory. But this does not make such rules useless; it merely makes them somewhat less than perfect.

We usually try to construct the codified rules so that they are "safe": so that adhering to them will not produce barbarisms, although they can occasionally be broken by someone who knows both what he is doing and why he is doing it. The rules of grammar and punctuation are linguistic safety rules. As with industrial safety rules or the rules of safe driving, rare situations can occasionally arise where a prudent man will violate the rules, to avoid the very catastrophes they were supposed to prevent. The point is that any such violations should be conscious, reasoned, and defensible, not merely reckless.

While few native speakers of English have any serious difficulty with its grammar, obscurities remain common in much that is written, and such obscurities probably arise most frequently from failing to observe what might be called the *spirit of grammar,* which is even more restrictive than its rules: the grammatical structure of a sentence should not only be "correct"; it should also reflect and reinforce the pattern of thought that the sentence is intended to convey. Such matters of intent are extremely difficult to codify, although we made an attempt to treat them in chapter III. But these matters cannot even be approached without a terminology, a grammar, that will enable us to name and discuss the elements of structure within a sentence. Conversely, a familiarity with the detailed technical structures of English sentences will often help a writer to see why his words do not seem to embody his true thoughts, and will frequently aid him in devising an appropriate cure.

SENTENCE CORE

NOUN AND ARTICLE — VERB

Essential to a complete English sentence are only two words: a noun (or pronoun) as subject, and a finite verb (a verb limited by the conditions of its use in person, number, and time) as predicate. The noun may be either common or proper (a specific designation capitalized), either concrete or abstract, designating something having physical existence on the one hand, or on the other a mental concept without physical existence. Associated with it may be one of the articles, *a (an)* or *the*. These simple monosyllables give much trouble to foreigners learning English, and are frequently not used correctly by native speakers, who often are puzzled (or should have been) which to use or whether to use neither. A knowledge of their origin is a valuable clue to their proper use. The indefinite article *a (an)* is from the same Anglo-Saxon source *(ān)* as the English word *one*, of which it is merely a weakened form. *An apple* is therefore *one apple*, with a little less emphasis on its singleness. The definite article *the* is from the same ultimate source (*thaet* in one of its forms) as the English demonstrative pronouns *that* and *this* (plurals *those* and *these*). *The apple* is therefore a particular (definite) apple, pointed out only somewhat less strongly than *this apple* or *that apple*. The form without either article, simply *apple* or *apples,* particularly common in the plural, is generic, signifying neither a single specimen chosen as sample nor any particular individualized apple or apples.

In our two-word sentence (or any sentence) the verb will be finite, limited by its subject in person and number, but unchanging in its form for person and number (except for the verb *to be*) with the exception of the third person singular indicative in *s* (as *has* from *have*) — and limited in time (or tense) by its form (*have,* or *has,* for the present, *had* for the past, and so on). The verb will be intransitive, for in order to make it transitive, we should have to supply a third word (a noun or pronoun as object for the verb to perform its action or have its effect upon); and it will be in the active voice, for only with a third word (a form of the verb *to be*) could we make it passive. It will not be a copulative verb, acting as =, for then also it would require a third word signifying what the subject is the equivalent of or a quality of the subject (its complement).

Since this behavior of the English verb and its related subject and object, or complement, is vitally important to the structure of an English sentence and about the most complicated aspect of it, let us have a look at the effects it can produce, taking the liberty of introducing a third word (in addition to the articles).

1. *The man paid.* (Third person, singular. Verb intransitive and past tense.)
2. *The man paid a bill.* (The same, except transitive verb with the object *bill.*)
3. *The bill was paid.* (Third person, singular. Verb past tense and passive voice.)

Note that in 3 the object of the verb in the active voice has become the subject of the passive verb, with the result that the subject is now called passive, because it performs no action. The agent of the action (*man* in 2) has been completely suppressed. This is the principal function of the passive voice, to suppress or ignore agency. *For all other purposes, and especially where agency is to be expressed, the active voice is preferred.* It is the common form of expression, for subjects as active agents are generally more important than objects.

Now let us consider the copulative verb, the verb which is intransitive but still requires a noun (or pronoun or adjective) to complete its meaning. *To be* is the most common of them, but there are others, and let us take another.

Mr. Kennedy became president.
Mr. Kennedy   =   president.

The object of a transitive verb will never be the equivalent in meaning of the subject of that verb (except when it is a reflexive pronoun, forms ending in *self, myself,* or plural *selves, themselves*), but the noun or pronoun complement always expresses equivalence. The adjective complement likewise designates an attribute of the subject. *The room was beautiful* is semantically equivalent to *The beautiful room.*

One more possible aspect of the simple sentence core needs to be considered, the objective complement. Sometimes the transitive verb requires completing with a noun, pronoun, or adjective in addition to its object:

The voters elected Mr. Kennedy president.

President is here the objective complement, so called because it is now the equivalent of the direct object of the verb *(Mr. Kennedy)*. Similarly the adjective objective complement presents an attribute of the object of the verb — *The man painted the house white.* When an active verb is put into passive form and its former passive object thus becomes its passive subject, the objective complement of the active form becomes the subjective complement of the now intransitive verb — *Mr. Kennedy was elected president.*

VERB TENSES

Time relations of the sentence are controlled principally by the verb, and when they are not actually thus controlled, the verb must accommodate itself to them, through its tense. English *tense* is from Old French *tens,* developed from Latin *tempus,* time. Thus the tense of a verb is essential to time relations. Little trouble can arise among the appropriately designated simple tenses, present, past, and future (the last formed with *shall* or *will* as auxiliaries). Although *shall* and *will* are not used interchangeably, grammarians have long since given up adherence to the old rule of *shall* in the first person and *will* in the second and third for simple futurity. This always required exceptions, and usage has introduced so many that the rule has been abandoned. But no systematizing of present unstable usage has seemed possible, and meanwhile the old

rule serves as a rough guide, with exceptions introduced intuitively.

It is in the perfect tenses (*perfect* from Latin
perfectus, done thoroughly, completed), present perfect, past perfect, and future perfect, that confusion
arises. The key to correct use is to remember the
meaning of *perfect,* completed. The present perfect
tense (with *have, has,* as auxiliary) refers to action
completed at the present time. It thus covers the
same general time area as the past tense, and the
two are used somewhat interchangeably, the principal
difference being that because the present perfect
stresses completion of the action, it suggests recent
completion (compare *He stole* with *He has stolen*).
Furthermore, a peculiarity of the past tense is that it
expresses no completion of the action. *He stole* in no
way suggests that "he" is not still stealing, so that if
completion of the action is to be established in the
general past, remote or recent, the present perfect must
be used.

The past perfect and future perfect tenses are not
interchangeable with any others and have well-defined
uses. The past perfect (with *had* as auxiliary) is used
for action that was completed at an established time
in the past. (For example, *When he came here, he
had stolen.*) The tense is thus used only in a context
dominated by past time. Similarly, the future perfect
(formed with *shall* or *will* and *have*) refers to action
complete at an established time in the future, and is
thus used only in a context dominated by the future.
(For example, *He will have lost his opportunity* makes
sense only with reference to some established future
time.)

Although one can state categorically that the past

perfect always accompanies only the past tense in English, one cannot similarly state that the future perfect always accompanies only the future tense, because of two characteristics of the language. One of these is that time is not invariably determined by verb tenses, but sometimes by temporal adverbs or adverbial phrases or clauses (*then, now, when that day comes,* and the like). The other characteristic, illustrated in the last example, is that of using the present tense, not only for past action, as in the "historical present," but also for future action, especially but not exclusively in dependent clauses. (*We leave next week. We shall then have sold our house.*) Even more commonly used with a future meaning is the present imperfect (discussed below), *We are leaving next week.* Whatever the complications, however, the general principles here set forth will, if each case is sufficiently pondered, guide the writer to proper choice of tenses. He need only bear in mind that however a past or future time has been established, the past perfect tense refers to action that has occurred before the established past time, and the future perfect tense to action that will occur between the present and the established future time.

A construction sometimes considered a tense because the distinction it makes is made by tense in other languages is not actually a tense in English, for it exists in all tenses and therefore does not itself control the time of occurrence of an action. It is actually the imperfect (uncompleted) "aspect" of the verb, contrasted with the perfect (completed) "aspect" on which the perfect tenses are based. Often called the progressive or durative form of the verb, it is constructed with *to be* and the present participle of the verb in question, to express continuing action, action without termination. *(He is, was, has been, etc., driving.)*

In the table below are demonstrated the time relations of English tenses. The vertical line represents present time, the area to the left of it the past, and the area to the right of it the future. The present perfect tense alludes to action completed before the present time, the past perfect to action completed at a time established in the past, and the future perfect to action to be completed at a time established in the future.

TIME RELATIONS IN ENGLISH TENSES

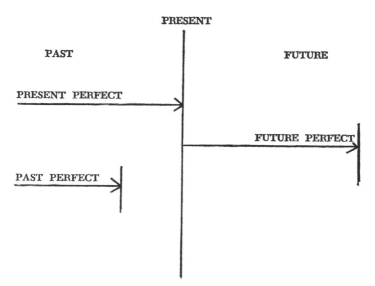

The subject of tense should not be dropped without admonition that continuance in the same tense should always be practiced except where the time reference changes. Tense shows time, and should change only to reflect time change, but should change then.

Besides time relations through tense changes, verbs show the manner of an action, the spirit in which a remark is made and is to be received, through changes of mood (or mode). The common mood of direct assertion is the indicative. Modern English has also inherited an imperative and a subjunctive mood. The imperative mood, used only in the second person and in the present tense (generally with no expression of the subject except to increase emphasis), is the mood of command. The subjunctive mood (so called because it is usually sub-joined, or subordinated, to another statement) expresses doubt, uncertainty, even improbability or impossibility. It still preserves some inflectional difference from the indicative, though it is gradually doing so to a less and less degree. In most verbs the omission from the third person singular of the form ending in *s* that distinguishes the third person singular indicative is the only inflectional difference of the subjunctive, and even that distinction is now less common than it once was, since we are much more likely to use an auxiliary as sign of the subjunctive (not *If he come*, but *If he should come*).

The conservative verb *to be* presents the principal problem in use of the subjunctive mood, and even *to be* has now pretty well lost its distinctive present subjunctive form of *be* in conditional clauses (*If it be so*). The past tense, extended to the present (*were* in all forms), still, however, makes a necessary distinction between what is definitely so and what is not, in the "contrary to fact" construction (*If I were you*). This is an essential grammatical distinction of the inflected subjunctive. The mood is also regularly used in *that* noun clauses expressing a wish, supposition, or proposal, where its correct use seems to cause most writers no trouble *(We advised that he be more careful).*

In addition to these historically inherited moods, Modern English has developed several auxiliary verbs used in present and past tenses before the infinitives of other verbs (regularly without the *to* sign of the infinitive) with a modal effect. Among its many uses the verb *do* thus serves as imperative and also as a means of emphasis *(I do believe him).* *May* and *can* are thus used, somewhat confusingly and even confusedly, as expressions, respectively, of permission and ability, and *shall* and *will,* in addition to their uses as auxiliaries of the future and future perfect tenses, are also used to express determination and volition. *(They shall not pass. I will do as I please.)*

Formerly, simple futurity was distinguished from determination by using for the future *shall* in the first person and *will* in the second and third, and using for determination direct substitution of one verb for the other (*will* in the first person and *shall* in the second and third). This distinction was not ever strictly observed, however, probably under the principal influence of the almost universal elision of the forms in speech, in which, of course, they are of common occurrence (*I'll, you'll, we'll, they'll,* etc.). In these daily expressions the word elided might reasonably be either *shall* or *will. I'll,* of frequent occurrence in everyone's speech, even suggests by its sounds *will* rather than *shall.* Thus, in speech the full form was obscured, so that speakers may well both have lost the habit of making any distinction and have come to feel that the unaccustomed use of either form in full was itself an expression of determination.

Particularly interesting and serviceable is the development of the past tenses of *may, can, shall,* and *will* into both independent and auxiliary verbs at the same time that they continue to serve in their original capacities as past tenses. Not only are *might, could, should,* and *would* the past tenses of *may, can, shall,* and *will,* but each of them has a separate auxiliary function of its own. Each has the same general meaning as its present-tense form, but always when it is serving as an independent verb or an auxiliary, it has a weakened intensity. It is as though the remoteness of time suggested by the past-tense use had blurred intention and created remoteness of purpose. (Compare: *I may go. I might go. — I can go. I could go. — I shall go. I should go. — I will go. I would go.*) All four of these auxiliaries of hesitation, but particularly *should* and *would* as less intense forms of *shall* and *will,* have come generally into use to form conditionals expressive of uncertainty or rejection, and have thus contributed strongly, as mentioned above, to the diminishing use of the inherited inflectional subjunctive. Consider:

> *If I might speak, I should be believed.*
> *If I could speak, I should be believed.*
> *If I should speak, I would be believed.*
> *If I would speak, I should be believed.*

Note that all these forms of rejectional or hesitant condition call for appropriate auxiliaries in the main clause as well as in the conditional clause.

In still another use *should* becomes practically a synonym of *must* and *ought* as expressive of obligation. Like *should, must* and *ought* are etymologically past tenses. The present tense of *must (mote)* is no longer in use, and the present tense of *ought* has become two different and quite separate verbs *(owe* and *own)*. All three former past tenses have become now independent verbs and auxiliaries of obligation. They are uninflected, but with *ought* the sign of the infinitive *(to)* is always used, often even when the infinitive itself is not expressed *(I ought to)*, whereas all other true modal auxiliaries regularly omit it.

As is usually true of synonyms, the three auxiliaries are not exactly alike in the degree and nature of the obligation they express. From its origin (past tense of *owe)* one would expect *ought* to express strongest obligation, and it does imply a debt of conscience, but perhaps because man so frequently frustrates his conscience, it suggests the least intention of fulfilment of obligation, even when supported, as its weakness seems frequently to require, in such a phrase as *I really ought*. Strongest obligation is expressed by *must; should* is rather neutral. But the weakest in intention of all these auxiliaries is *might*, which, as though influenced by *mite*, almost denies intention — a very useful word for a highly doubtful assertion.

Modern English has no optative mood, as Anglo-Saxon had. But it has many verbs of optative meaning *(wish, desire, want, crave, yearn,* and *would,* as in *Would that he were here!)*. It also has three synonymous verbs which, when used with a following infinitive, have a weakly optative meaning. These are *let, permit,* and *allow.* (The infinitive after *let* usually lacks the *to* sign — *Let us go.)* The optative significance is sometimes strong, as in *Let us pray,* but often so weak as not to suggest a wish or desire, but to be merely acquiescent or non-prohibitory, as in *Let him do as he chooses.* In lacking an optative mood, then, English is not deprived of great variety in expression of the optative feeling. But in a manner generally characteristic of English in the simplification of its inflections, it has lost a classifiable optative, and has gained the power to express optative feeling in many shades of meaning.

Pronoun

Pronouns perform the function of nouns, and each one commonly represents a specific noun, its "antecedent." Some pronouns, however, notably interrogative and indefinite pronouns, have no expressed antecedents (referents). The purpose of an interrogative pronoun is to seek an antecedent in the answer, and an indefinite pronoun is so called precisely because its reference is vague and general, its antecedent unidentifiable. Sometimes pronouns not generally considered indefinite are correctly used thus, notably the compound relative pronouns ending in "ever" (*whoever, whatever,* etc.) and also sometimes the simple uncompounded *who, what,* and the like. Of the personal pronouns only *it* and *we* are properly so used; *they* should not be used indefinitely, as it too frequently is. The word *it* carries its indefiniteness in certain perfectly acceptable English contexts to such an extreme that the word in such uses can hardly be considered a pronoun: in the familiar remark "It is raining" one would be at a loss to state what is raining except rain. The second-personal *you,* like third-personal *they,* is much overused indefinitely. It should be reserved as the person of direct address. Where a writer is tempted to use *you* or *they* impersonally, the first person plural *we* may often be used correctly

and effectively. Its antecedent may then be the whole
human species, or any group of persons, or even only
one person in the somewhat pontificating "editorial
we."

The truly referent pronouns are the personal, relative, and demonstrative ones. The demonstrative pronouns are simplicity itself: only *this* and *that* (with
their plurals *these* and *those*), existing in Modern
English only in these forms. Their only difference is
that *this (these)* refers to the close at hand and *that
(those)* to the more remote. As pronominal adjectives
they may perform as both parts of speech, as in the
last two words of the second sentence in this paragraph, and since their reference should always be
unmistakably clear, the insertion of an appropriate
noun after them (by no means always necessary) will
strengthen a weak reference. Personal and relative
pronouns should also establish strong and unambiguous reference. It is not enough that the reader be
able to trace the reference. The reference should be
so unquestionably apparent that the reader need never
pause to consider it. Nothing requires more care than
precise reference of pronouns. The writer often has
only in his mind the referent that he thinks exists on
paper. He should check to be sure.

Of all pronouns the personal have most tenaciously
retained their inflection, a common situation in languages because of the frequent use of personal pronouns in basic speech. Although some forms have
been dropped or considerably altered and a few added,
English personal pronouns are today not greatly different from their Anglo-Saxon counterparts in number or
richness of representation, especially if we include the
now archaic but completely intelligible *thou, thine,*

and *thee*. The forms *mine* (of which *my* is only a shortened form), *me, we, us, he, his,* and *him* are virtually unchanged, and it is easy to recognize *I* in Anglo-Saxon *ic, our* in Anglo-Saxon *ūre, you* in Anglo-Saxon *ēow, your* in Anglo-Saxon *ēower, her* in Anglo-Saxon *hire,* and *it* in Anglo-Saxon *hit.* *Its* is a late development from *it,* not yet common in Shakespeare's day. *They, their,* and *them* are of Old Norse origin, and the source of *she* is much debated. The dictionaries, without general approval of linguists, accept *sēo,* an Anglo-Saxon feminine demonstrative, as probably confused with *hēo,* the Anglo-Saxon form for *she.*

The use of personal pronouns, though complicated, is familiar to any careful speaker of the language, all of whom know that their still varied inflection is a trap for the unwary who are accustomed to the almost uninflected English nouns. Change of form to correspond to person and case is not a familiar experience in English, familiar as personal pronouns are. We meet the situation elsewhere only in the case changes of the relative pronoun *who, whose, whom,* the misuse of which is a source of glee to the grammatically well-informed and of frequent embarrassment to the weak grammatical aspirant. *The clue to this riddle lies, of course, always in the use of the pronoun in its own clause.*

Parts of Speech

CONJUNCTION — PREPOSITION

We have now dealt with the noun, verb, and pronoun, and treated the adjective as complement. Leaving the modifiers (adjective and adverb) for later treatment, we can quite expeditiously dispose of the other parts of speech (interjection, preposition, and conjunction). The interjection by definition does not enter into the structure of a sentence: its function is to interrupt with a burst of strong feeling, to express emotion rather than thought. The vocative, actually a case, not a part of speech, it may be remarked parenthetically, is also thrust into the sentence, and in its function of calling for attention directly upon the person, persons, or sometimes thing or things, addressed has only slightly more relation than the interjection to the sentence whose structure it actually interrupts.

Prepositions and conjunctions, although they perform quite different functions, are nonetheless both connectives. True conjunctions only connect, but many of them are so adverbial in significance that they are called conjunctive adverbs. Prepositions, words many of which are also used as adverbs or conjunctions, form phrases (to be discussed below) by connecting a substantive (noun, pronoun, or other noun equivalent), their objects, to some other part of the sentence.

Both prepositions and conjunctions are so numerous as to defy listing, and their great variety both enriches the power of the language for subtle distinction of meaning and puzzles the insensitive or uninformed, especially adults first learning the language. We can reasonably insist that a child say "at home" instead of "to home," but less reasonably insist that he say "in my opinion" rather than "by my opinion" or "under my opinion." Distinction between *since, for, because,* and *as* as causal conjunctions requires considerable subtlety, a distinction greatly complicated by the common use of *since* as adverb and preposition and the more common use of *for* as a preposition with an extensive variety of meanings. As for *as,* its frequent occurrence in varied senses and functions almost completely nullifies its usefulness as a causal conjunction, lest the reader be at least temporarily confused by accepting it as performing another function. Or let the reader try to distinguish satisfactorily between the adversative pairs of prepositions *below — above, under — over, beneath — upon,* and the various shufflings of their elements. He will then admit that delicate perceptions are required to express precise relations of his thought by judicious choice among the multifarious possibilities presented by English prepositions and conjunctions. Choice is often inhibited by idiomatic fixations that usage has established, seemingly more or less arbitrary conventions of association. The writer must be familiar with these, and since the function of these parts of speech is wholly to express relations of thought, accurate selection among them is a most critically significant aspect of good writing.

Methods of Grammatical Elaboration

Our original three- or four-word sentence, consisting of subject, verb, and possibly object and/or complement, can be extended or elaborated in three ways: (1) by modification (alteration) of its parts, (2) by the substitution for nouns or modifiers of whole groups of words (phrases or dependent clauses that have their own well-defined grammatical structure), or (3) by compounding (doubling, or even tripling, quadrupling, etc.) any of its parts or its entire form in parallel structure by means of conjunctions. These methods of extending and elaborating the sentence are, of course, what make it such a supple and sophisticated instrument of expression. Each of them will be discussed in turn.

MODIFICATION

ADJECTIVE — ADVERB

Any structural element of a sentence, as distinct from mere connectives, may be modified (have its meaning affected or elaborated) by an adjective or an adverb ("to the verb," literally). The conventional distinction between the two, that an adjective modifies a noun or pronoun, and an adverb a verb, an adjective, or another adverb, is a classification of their uses particularly significant in English, which makes no other clear distinction between them, though a somewhat inadequate one. That adverbs sometimes modify no single specific word, but a whole phrase or clause, has long been recognized in English grammar (as in *Fortunately no one was injured),* though some grammarians extend this use unwarrantably by so classifying instances in which the adverb actually modifies the verb from a remote position, usually the beginning of the sentence. Unorthodox as the statement may appear, adverbs sometimes clearly modify prepositions. How else is one to explain such expressions as *The car was partly on and partly off the road* or *Just under one inch?* Coleridge, in *The Rime of the Ancient Mariner,* wrote:

> Almost upon the western wave
> Rested the broad bright Sun . . .

The caesura (natural pause in the line) after *upon* makes his meaning pretty certain, not that the sun very nearly stopped, "almost rested," on the wave, but that the precise place where it rested was "very nearly *on"* the wave. The adverb is a most versatile part of speech, and if grammar is to reflect actual use of the language, as it assuredly should, then it would seem wise to broaden the definition of an adverb to that part of speech which performs all single-word modification not performed by the adjective (modification of nouns and pronouns).

Some distinction between adjective and adverb in form is inherited from Anglo-Saxon and later habits of suffixing Anglo-Saxon *līc* (our *like,* weakened in this use to *-ly*) primarily in Anglo-Saxon in the formation of adjectives, but in later English usurped for forming adverbs from adjectives. Thus *sharply* = *sharp-like* and *deathly* = *death-like.* Common as such adverbs are, however, the *-ly* suffix is by no means an invariable "sign of the adverb," as witness the adjectives *goodly, lowly, worldly,* and many more, among which *low* can be used as an adverb, whereas *good* so used generally denotes illiteracy. With loss of Anglo-Saxon inflection of the adjective, English has lost any actual distinction in form between adjectives and adverbs. They are distinguishable only by their use. Yet many words, especially the adverbs in *-ly,* can be used in only one of the two ways, and care is needed to follow literate practice.

Adjectives and adverbs may, of course, be strengthened through degrees of comparison, and whether the comparative degree is to be formed with *-er* or *more* and the superlative with *-est* or *most* often requires delicate decision, where prevailing practice is one's only ultimate guide. Adverbs usually express degrees of comparison with *more* and *most,* though some, especially the "flat" adverbs that are felt to lack an admissible *-ly* ending, are compared like adjectives that use *-er* and *-est.*

Faulty comparison arises from failure to complete the comparison properly. The basis of comparison, what comparison is made to, must always be made apparent. The comparison must be fully stated unless it clearly refers to a basis already established by the context. As frequently expressed in advertisements, "best" or "better" means nothing unless the reader is informed "best" of what or "better" than what. Completion of comparisons also involves completion of such expressions as "The time interval is as great in the first instance as in the second, or greater." The proper form is here illustrated. The first of two comparisons of different degree should be completed. Then the second can be left incomplete because the basis of comparison is already established.

Without modifiers to enrich and elaborate meaning, any language would be a poor, strangled medium of communication, but modification adds a load that impedes the movement of the sentence, and precise choice of the word to be modified, by eliminating or reducing necessity for modification, decreases the load gratifyingly.

SUBSTITUTION

Grammatical substitution for the noun, adjective, or adverb of whole groups of words constructed for this purpose is above all else what makes adequate communication of complicated thought possible. Such groups of words are either phrases or dependent (subordinate) clauses, better considered separately. A phrase, though two of the three ways of constructing one require a verb form, contains no finite verb. A clause does.

Phrases are formed with prepositions, with infinitives, or with participles. Prepositional phrases, to begin with them, are formed with a preposition and its object, a substantive (noun or noun substitute), which is always, it should be carefully noted in use of inflected pronouns, in the accusative or objective case, and which may be modified to any reasonable extent. Though prepositional phrases may be used as nouns (as in *To the house is the shortest way*), their more normal use is as modifiers, either adjective or adverb. They alone extend the possibilities of communication vastly.

One of the verbals (verb forms) used to construct phrases is the infinitive. The Anglo-Saxon infinitive, like the Latin one, was originally identified by its ending, in Anglo-Saxon *an,* which in Middle English (the Middle Ages) became *en* and then just *e.* In Middle English many words ended in *e,* the only vowel remnant of the fairly complex Anglo-Saxon declensions (although *s* survived as the only consonant to provide our usual plural and possessive), and the final *e*'s were generally pronounced. Eventually even the *e* was dropped as an infinitive ending, and while it survived it was not a very distinctive ending among so many *e*'s, so that the habit arose of preceding an infinitive with the words "for to," common practice in the late Middle Ages, and familiar today in the nursery rhymes of Baby Bunting *(For to get a rabbit skin)* and Simple Simon *(for to catch a whale).* This "sign of the infinitive" was shortened in Modern English to just "to," so that English infinitives are now generally designated by this introductory particle. But not uncommonly it is dispensed with, and we must then recognize the infinitive purely by its function in the sentence.

Its function may be that of a noun, an adjective, or an adverb in any of the normal uses of these parts of speech. As a verb form, though non-finite (or infinite), the infinitive may itself have either a subject or an object, or both. *(He told his assistant to bake the material.)* Both subject and object are in the accusative case, important, of course, only when inflected pronouns are involved, but highly important then *(He told me to help him).* The infinitive may be either active or passive (with *to be* as auxiliary), and in either of these voices may be either present (sharing the time of the main verb with which it occurs, whatever the tense of that verb) or perfect (with *have* as auxiliary and showing completion of its action prior to the time of its main verb, like a perfect tense).

The only other way to form phrases is with participles of verbs. Participles may be present (ending in *-ing*), past (normally ending in *-ed,* but having special forms in "irregular" verbs, *lost, been, swum,* etc., mostly survivals of Anglo-Saxon "strong" verbs), or perfect (with *having* as auxiliary before the past participle). Any of these three forms may also be passive in voice (with *to be* as auxiliary). The present participle expresses action accompanying that of its main verb, and the past participle action initiated before the time of its main verb. The perfect participle, as would be expected, refers to action completed before the time of its main verb. Participles may be used with all tenses. These time and voice references of participles, and of infinitives, make possible delicate identifications of time and agency in their adjustments to action of a finite verb.

Participles perform the functions of adjectives or nouns. Used as nouns they are called, in the terminology of Latin grammar, gerunds, but since only its functioning as a noun makes a participle a gerund, the distinction seems unnecessary. Participles, whether used as adjectives or nouns, may, as verb forms, have objects and complements as well as modifiers. The gerund (but not the adjectival participle*), like the infinitive, not uncommonly also takes a subject in the accusative case *(We saw him thoughtlessly moving the apparatus).*

One of the writer's most frequent problems is that of arranging modifiers in a sentence so that they will be readily associated with their referents. This problem is most acute in using phrasal modifiers of all three types, prepositional, infinitive, and participial. The reader's thought flows along the sentence not unlike an electric current along a wire. An open circuit breeds trouble. More voltage is required to bridge the gap, and sparks of irritation may well accompany the reader's attempts to overcome the resistance he has encountered. Especially guilty of creating these irritations, or downright misunderstandings when the mind flows the wrong way, are participles.

Because when used as adjectives, they can have no subjects, yet are verbals expressing action, it is essential that the performer of the action they express be clearly indicated. For the adjectival participle this function must be performed by its referent, and in general such

---

* The participle, however, takes a subject in the nominative case in absolute constructions (See pp. 37 and 136).

a participle must refer clearly to the referent performing the action. Occasionally, either active or passive participles express action which has no specific agent, may be performed by an indefinite agent (for example, *The work was well done considering the circumstances),* and then, of course, the action cannot possibly be assigned to any specific agent. Failure to establish a reasonable and efficient referent for an adjectival participle whose agency is definite produces the "dangling participle," dangling like a loose wire in an electric circuit, likely to make an unfortunately ludicrous or damaging contact. The substantive participle (or gerund) becomes a modifier only as the object in a prepositional phrase. Then it is subject to the same necessity as the adjectival participle of having for the phrase a referent that is an appropriate agent for its action, unless its action is general, a much more common situation in the use of these gerundive participles *(In performing this task, great care must be exercised).* The problem often arises with any modifying infinitive or prepositional phrase. In fact, all modifiers may "dangle" in positions dangerously remote from their proper referents, and dangerously close to improper ones.

SUBSTITUTION BY CLAUSE

A clause, even though dependent, is a potential sentence, for it contains a complete subject and a predicate complete with finite verb. It is made dependent usually by the word that introduces it, a subordinating conjunction, conjunctive adverb, or relative pronoun, and occasionally simply by its position. A dependent clause is therefore a whole sentence, slightly altered,

used like a noun, an adjective, or an adverb.   Clauses
are best classified according to their use.

Noun clauses may go anywhere that a noun may.
They generally enter properly introduced by a con-
junctional signal that serves little purpose except the
important one of announcing the presence of the
clause, but they occasionally burst in unannounced
(I told him I would see him later)*. They may trail
along with them, as may any dependent clause, modifiers of all sorts, adjectives, adverbs, phrases, and even
other dependent clauses, although too much conges-
tion of clause within clause can eventually lead to
hopeless confusion — a danger to be avoided with scrupulous caution, especially when clauses of similar construction modify each other in succession.

All clauses introduced by relative pronouns are adjective clauses, for the pronouns must, of course, have
unmistakable substantive antecedents, better a single
noun or pronoun, for the habit of referring with a
pronoun to an idea distributed among many words can
prove dangerously degenerative of clear thinking on
the part of both writer and reader. All adjective clauses
are not, conversely, strictly relative clauses, for adjective clauses are not always introduced by a relative
pronoun, often by a relative adverb (. . . *the point
where they meet,* . . . *the time when he came,* etc.).
The true relative pronouns are *who, which,* and *that;
what* also has complex uses that are of a relative nature,
and can often be suitably substituted for *that which.
Who* is preferred in reference to persons, though *that*
is gaining favor, perhaps because of the troublesome

---

* *Him* is here an indirect object. (See p. 135).

inflection of *who,* the proper case of which *(who, whose, whom) depends always upon its use in its own clause.* Number and, when personal pronouns are antecedents of relative pronouns, person, are determined for the relative pronoun, and hence the verb it takes, by the number (and person) of its antecedent. *That* is generally preferable to *which* (never used for persons) in restrictive (limiting or identifying) clauses, but the suggestion cannot be slavishly adhered to, for *that* is not always idiomatically applicable. Sometimes the relative pronoun is omitted *(He is the man I told you about).*

Adverbial clauses would probably take the prize from relative clauses in a popularity contest. Both are extremely common, but relative clauses, introduced by the few relative pronouns, all of which are quite devoid of meaning, cannot function with the infinite variety of adverbial clauses, a variety as great as the inexhaustible list of subordinating conjunctions that introduce them. These words express almost every conceivable shade of meaning in categories as diverse as time, place, cause, result, purpose, condition, concession, manner, limitation, and the like. Adverbial clauses are sometimes in elliptical form *(When backing out of a garage . . .* for *When one is backing out of a garage . . .).* Then, with their subjects suppressed, they are not easily distinguished from adjectival participles, especially at the beginning of a sentence, the preferred position for adverbial clauses, and the same care must then be taken with them as with participles to assure that agency is clearly expressed, either by filling in the ellipsis or implying the agency clearly in the rest of the sentence.

Compounding is co-ordination that results in parallel structures. Within sentences it involves doubling, tripling, or even further multiplying a sentence element, often with the aid of a co-ordinating conjunction. Parallelism is practiced instinctively by good writers, for it is characteristic of clear and orderly thinking. It co-ordinates thought and the expression of it wherever co-ordination is appropriate. It takes the form of series, and requires that two or more concepts of similar import in the context be expressed in the same grammatical construction, so that within these constructions part corresponds to part, and the constructions themselves are twins, triplets, and the like. It requires that, wherever within a sentence two or more concepts should "fall into line," prepositional phrase shall match prepositional phrase, participial phrase match participial phrase, infinitive match infinitive, relative clause match relative clause, adverbial clause match adverbial clause, noun match noun, adjective match adjective, and adverb match adverb. It produces order, in much the same way that lining up men or equipment in ranks produces it. Parallelism from sentence to sentence can introduce the same kind of order into a paragraph. Within this paragraph much parallelism has been practiced, notably from sentence to sentence in the fourth through the seventh sentences, and within the sixth sentence.

Parallelism often requires repetition of key structural words (prepositions, conjunctions, relative pronouns, the "to" sign of the infinitive, articles if used at all in the structure, and the like), as the verb *match* is repeated in the sixth sentence of the above paragraph and *it* followed by the present tense of a verb begins each sentence from the fourth through the seventh. Such repetition is desirable rather than objectionable if it contributes to systematic, orderly progression of thought.

A greater danger than objectionable monotony in repetition of key words is the introduction of "false parallelism." So prevalent is parallelism that writers conscious of its value and using it instinctively sometimes try to force into parallel structure elements of their thought that are not actually co-ordinate, as in *At the turn of the century medical science was fighting disease by killing germs in human environment and by living outdoors as the best policy for its patients,* or in *Doctors visit their patients, the hospital, and medical meetings whenever they can.*

Conversely, a common failure to observe parallelism occurs in the notorious "and which" construction: use of a relative pronoun preceded by a co-ordinating conjunction when no co-ordinate relative pronoun precedes the conjunction, as in *He was a doctor giving excellent service to his patients, and whom everybody liked.* But the dangers of abusing parallelism should not deter any writer from utilizing, wherever it is appropriate, a device so conducive to orderly thinking.

MISCELLANEOUS CONSTRUCTIONS

A construction that might have been introduced into the discussion of our original "core sentence" did not seem significant enough to warrant complicating that early discussion with it. This is the indirect object in such a sentence as *We gave him the book. Book* is obviously the direct object of the verb, and *him* is the indirect object, designating the person in whose interest the act was performed. The inanimate may also be treated as the indirect object, as in *We gave the house a coat of paint.* The construction simulates an elided prepositional phrase from which "to" or "for" has been omitted, expressive of "to" or "for" whom or what the action was performed, not upon what (or whom) it was performed.

As the indirect object precedes another substantive, the appositive immediately follows one. It is a mere additional epithet, often modified, set beside another substantive to re-enforce or elaborate the first one. Frequently, with economy of phrasing, a relative clause can be reduced to an appositive. *(The top of the bolt, [which is] the round object visible from the front . . .)*

Another construction, somewhat similar to the appositive in its interjectory character, is the nominative absolute, a substantive in the nominative case (important for personal pronouns) used as subject of a participle, which is often itself modified. This absolute construction *(He having been tried, the jury brought in a verdict)* stands grammatically free from the rest of the sentence in which it is incorporated, generally at the beginning, and yet in thought it nevertheless constitutes a significant part of the sentence. It too can be used to reduce the bulk of a full clause.

Two other devices also concern the beginning of the sentence. One of these is the omission of the conditional *if*, often but not always at the beginning of the sentence, and the inversion of the verb and subject as an equivalent construction *(Had I known* for *If I had known).* Somewhat more rhetorical than the normal order, this construction offers a somewhat pleasant relief from it where appropriate.

The other device is the expletive, the use of a word,

usually *there* or *it,* to substitute as preliminary to the
actual subject, which is thus temporarily deferred to
appear later in the sentence. The device has value as
a means of emphasis and for variety of phrasing, but
it is greatly abused. Its habitual and continuous use
is a bad habit to be broken, especially when the construction merely serves to introduce a meaningless
subject that is modified by a relative clause to which is
relegated the real responsibility of affirmation *(There
is a method by which Jones found he could solve this
problem).* The main clause then becomes an empty
shell, robbed of its function of principal affirmation.

SENTENCE PATTERNS

Since the purpose of all grammatical manipulation
is to produce the well-built sentence, and the proof of
the pudding is in the satisfaction it gives, some remarks
should be made on the over-all sentence structure.
The common classification of sentences is, of course, as
(1) simple (containing only one clause and that the
main one), (2) complex (with at least one dependent
clause added), and (3) compound (with two or more
independent, or main, clauses). Since simple sentences, although they can, through extensive modification, become quite involved, are by definition basically
the least complicated and easiest to write, and since
compound sentences, unless also complex, are only
simple sentences co-ordinated, it is apparent that the
complex sentence is at the same time both most difficult
to compose and most satisfactory in the expression of a
thought at all complicated, for it both requires and
makes possible in its subordinations a weighed evaluation of the relative importance of its parts.

Simplicity is a virtue, and the common advice to

keep sentences short and simple has justification. But not all sentences can accomplish their purpose and remain short, and then the real art is, in Milton's phrase of the devil as serpent, to make intricate seem straight, for sometimes only a long sentence will adequately express the intricacies of a complicated thought. Complex thoughts cannot be simply expressed and lose a good deal of their significance when separated into parts. Long, complicated sentences are frequently the only form in which a long, complicated thought can be expressed, and the necessity then is to construct the required sentence with such attention to its grammatical conformation that it will convey to the reader smoothly and directly all of just exactly what the writer had in mind. A "mindful" of thought is precisely what the sentence is, or should be, for both writer and reader, a unit of achievement. The writer puts on paper in orderly arrangement as much of his thought — that unit of mental content — as his mind will comfortably accommodate with all parts in proper relation at one time, and the reader should be able, without undue effort, to find it there. Coleridge, who referred to grammar as "in essence no other than the laws of universal logic, applied to psychological materials," expressed excellently this essential problem for the writer of abstract thought as "that prospectiveness of mind, that surview, which enables a man to foresee the whole of what he is to convey, appertaining to any one point; and by this means so to subordinate and arrange the different parts according to their relative importance, as to convey it at once, and as an organized whole." In using long sentences, then, the writer must take special pains with their construction, and if he detects in a long sentence the least straining of the capacity of his own mind, he must relieve the greater strain on his reader's mind by breaking the material into separate sentences that are not more than a "mindful" for the average reader, at the same time assuring himself that he does not thereby sacrifice essential interrelations of his thought.

Very short sentences are effective for emphasis, as is also judicious use of the conspicuous beginning and end of sentences. Begin and end significantly is good advice for all units of composition, a whole work, a chapter, a paragraph, or a sentence.

Certain types of sentences are useful for special purposes. One such type is the simple or complex sentence called periodic (it can never be compound), in which no thought is grammatically complete until the end is reached. It holds thought suspended over its entire length. Occasionally used, it can vary the style, create suspense, and of course, emphasize the key that at the end eventually unlocks the meaning of the whole sentence. A type of compound sentence called balanced is an effective way to emphasize contrast. It consists of only two independent clauses (usually and better with no conjunction between them) constructed with scrupulous parallelism so that the same or contrasted words face each other in part for part of the sentence. Part answers part as in a detailed lay-out, and the contrasted words stand out against a background of repeated phrasing so sharply as to bring the contrasted meanings of the two clauses into clear focus. Samuel Johnson loved this compact construction: *In peace, children bury their parents; in war, parents bury their children.*

In any series in which climax is inherent, the climatic order of listing the items is, of course, preferred, and anticlimax, at any rate, should be avoided, unless a humorous effect is sought, for it will inevitably appear.

GRAMMAR VERSUS STRUCTURAL LINGUISTICS

We are aware of the attempts to supplant conventional grammar with the new devices of "structural linguistics" and "structural grammar," but we are not as yet greatly impressed with their usefulness in analyzing written language. Traditional grammar, it is maintained by proponents of these new approaches, was adopted from Latin and Greek grammar, and is ill-suited to a highly isolating language such as English because it was originally devised to analyze the structures of the highly inflected classical languages. Doubtless an unfortunately rigid resistance to the modifying of grammatical concepts to conform to language changes has sometimes been practiced by shortsighted grammarians more interested in preserving grammar than in linguistic development. But why tear the house down because the roof leaks? Roofs frequently have to be repaired to withstand heavy deluges. If grammatical concepts have been eroded under the poundings of natural linguistic development, they can perhaps be refashioned to bear adequately the new stresses they are subjected to. It seems, at any rate, unwise to abandon the dwelling until we have something better to live in than the structural linguists have yet been able to offer.

Structural linguistics, with its tools of "phoneme" and "morpheme" (not always letters and words), of "junctures" (pauses), and of "stress" and "tone," is more concerned with the spoken than with the written language, and seems as yet to have little relevance to composition. Writing, though unquestionably influenced by prevalent speech, is not speech, and thoughts can never be recorded on a page as they would be delivered in speech. The road from the eye to the brain is not the same as that from the ear to the brain. Thoughts and all their constituent parts must be so arranged on paper that the eye apprehends them quickly in all their relations to each other. Spelling is completely conventionalized, and therefore the recognition of a written word bears little relation to the subtle differences of sounds (its phonemes) that represent it in speech, often with many subtle variations, by a variety of perfectly competent speakers. A morpheme is as clearly recognized in traditional grammar as in structural linguistics, and better identified. Stress, tone, and juncture play only a minor role, if any, in reading that is not rendered orally, except where pauses conform to punctuation, as they frequently do not, and even then it is doubtful that the signal of the punctuation to the mind corresponds in any way to the pause it would elicit in oral reading.

The structural grammarians have attempted to build a new grammar on the structural linguists' concepts of the "immediate constituent," the distinction of subject from predicate, an indispensable first step in grammatical analysis, but not a very advancing stride, and of word classifications. The classification recognizes words of Classes 1, 2, 3, and 4, which are merely, in disguise, nouns, verbs, adjectives, and adverbs. The remaining parts of speech active in the sentence are called "structure" or "function" words — pronouns, prepositions, and conjunctions — all of which do, of course, show relationship, and therefore have, though pronouns only in part, as a main function determination of relationships within the sentence.

All of the seven parts of speech that enter into sentence structure are thus represented in structural grammar, but in a somewhat myopic way. The structural grammarian seems to concentrate his attention, as though fascinated by it, upon the distinction between subject and predicate, and to be loath to go beyond it. He recognizes that all parts of speech — though he avoids calling them that except when he must to become intelligible at all — are somehow involved in both subject and predicate, but he shudders at the prospect of having to define the function of each of them. He seems eager to convince himself that their functions are insignificant, that they simply contribute in some way to the composition of the undoubtedly essential subject and predicate. He therefore seems to be obscuring grammar, as though he were ashamed of it, rather than clarifying it.

It is the conviction of the present writers that conventional grammar is a valuable heritage, that it defines the relationships of words to each other in establishing meaning better than any other system yet devised, that it enables us to discuss, in almost full generality, various recurring constructions and interrelations in language. Without grammatical concepts one cannot identify or discuss defective or awkward constructions. Without grammatical terminology one cannot describe the conventions of punctuation.

We feel that any grammar should be both truly structural and truly functional, and thoroughly so, that it should analyze the part each word plays in conveying an intended meaning. Grammar thus becomes the key to meaning as meaning is the key to grammar.

Words must be functional and thoughts must be structural. A word that has no function in the structure of a thought, does not belong to it in some meaningful way, should be eliminated from its expression, and conversely the function of a word can be determined only by defining what it contributes to the thought of which it is a part. Under this conviction, we have attempted to sketch the present state of conventional grammar as explanation of the structures functioning in our language.

Although grammar, like the dictionary, cannot prescribe usage, but merely describe it, it can offer the best possible description of the logical relations of words, of the constructions by means of which language communicates complicated thought.

A FUNCTIONAL VIEW OF GRAMMAR

Yet, because grammar is functional, it is quite possible to study function instead of parts of speech. In fact, words are established as parts of speech only by the function they perform, and hence function determines parts of speech, a classification by means of which both the function and behavior of individual words can be studied. Because function alone does not individualize words or explain their behavior as units, but merely classifies them, it seems to us far less precise to confine attention to function than to accept the functional classification that is the foundation (but only the foundation) of conventional grammar and proceed with conventional grammar into the study of the unit behavior through which each word performs its function.

But it may well be that some consideration of function will serve as an over-all view of grammar, throwing a spotlight on it from a different angle.   If we again omit interjections, words perform in a sentence just five principal functions:

1) *Designation* is performed by all nouns and other substantives, including gerunds, infinitives, and noun clauses. This is the simplest and obviously most fundamental function of words, to designate something.

2) *Assertion and interrogation* (which is a tentative or conditional form of assertion) are performed by finite verbs.   So essential is the verb to interrogation that questions in English, unless introduced by a pronoun or adverb *(who, which, what, why, where, when, how,* etc.) to indicate the precise nature of the expected answer, are regularly introduced by a verb, usually in auxiliary form.   Assertion is, of course, made in all clauses, dependent or independent, and therefore a finite verb, either expressed or understood, is essential to all clauses, the heart or power plant of every predicate, the only means of making a statement.

3) *Modification* is the function of adjectives and adverbs, and of phrases and clauses substituted for them. By this device the meaning of more primary words is altered or qualified to secure greater precision.

4) *Reference* is the principal function of pronouns, but it can also be accomplished by other words. Reference bridges context to make contact with other individual words or groups of words, usually antecedent, but sometimes post-cedent.   Pronouns acquire their meaning from their referents, or antecedents, and serve always to call these to mind.   The same kind of contact can be established across context by repetition of words.   Any words or groups of words may be so

repeated. Nouns are especially subject to such repetition, or substitution of a synonym, especially when accompanied by the definite article, the pronominal origin and function of which was explained above.*
Parallelism is based on a similar sort of repetition. Reference signals contacts throughout context.

5) *Connection* is the special function of prepositions and conjunctions. They are link words. Because they link, their position is an important aspect of their function. They do not bridge context, but establish contact between words adjacent to them. A preposition always introduces its phrase, except on occasions when it is separated from its object and placed at the end of the sentence or clause for emphasis, and the phrase must stand close to what it modifies.

Both prepositions and conjunctions (but particularly prepositions through their great variety) not only link adjacent elements, but also define the nature of the relation that exists between them. In this respect, too, connection differs from reference, which generally serves only as a reminder of its referent in a somewhat remote position.

This cross-harrowing of the ground more thoroughly turned over in our discussion of conventional grammar may serve to lighten the soil, but as a substitute for that deeper plowing it obviously just scratches the surface. Function is important, but a study of it alone leaves untouched the deeper aspects of a word's alteration and behavior while it is functioning, which conventional grammar reveals.

---

* P. 110.

VIII

PUNCTUATION

Origins and Purpose

Systematic punctuation arose among the first printers, those of the fifteenth century. Earlier calligraphy did not even distinguish one word from another with spaces. Each line was filled with a continuous string of joined letters, which, though they spelled words, gave no indication of where each word ended and a new one began. Early English manuscripts did, in general, separate words with spaces, but scribes were not always careful about the spacing. They did not even distinguish sentences with capital letter and period. Periods and capital letters were inserted from time to time, but the capital letters were just decorative, and what may have been the function of the periods, if other than decorative, is a mystery. The modern printed representations of early texts that we read have been edited for us, and punctuated for or by printers, to make them conform to our conception of a book.

The man who first systematized punctuation was the fifteenth-century Italian printer who in general contributed most to the invention of the modern printed book, as distinct from a printed imitation of a medieval manuscript, the Venetian, Manutius Aldus. At his press, italic type was also developed for regular use, as we use roman type. His system of punctuation was quickly adopted by other printers, and is the basis of our present system. But punctuation, from its origin among the printers, has undergone considerable evolution, and has adapted itself to each of the languages in which it is used, so that the system of punctuation prevalent in any one language cannot be used in any other.

The system used by English printers has also evolved, so that the punctuation of earlier centuries is not that of today. English punctuation reached a high point of elaboration in the nineteenth century, when very "close" punctuation prevailed. The comma, semicolon, and colon were then considered to have climactic values such that each succeeding mark was stronger (signaled a more distinct change of thought) than the marks below it in the hierarchy. Against this elaborate punctuation our own century has rebelled, and has developed a "loose" punctuation that economizes in the use of the same conventional marks. In consequence, just as the punctuation of other languages will not serve to guide us, neither will the English punctuation even of the last century.

Punctuation has always been highly conventionalized, and our punctuation, too, is highly conventional. Though the system has been subjected to change, and may change further, it is hard to believe that the present tendency to minimize punctuation will be carried much further. Indeed, some authorities on the subject seem already to have carried the minimizing too far. Yet one cannot deplore our departure from the excessive punctuation of the nineteenth century. We have developed, when our conventions are properly preserved, a punctuation that is not only economical, but also entirely adequate, and that, without being at all obtrusive, serves well its purpose of delineating the grammatical structure of sentences.

But it should always be borne in mind that all punctuation is conventional. Just as our conventionalized spelling (a fairly recent development in language) ensures that generally only one combination of letters in a fixed order shall represent any one word, so the marks of punctuation we use must always have the same significance for all readers and writers. Unless every reader of a given writer interprets his punctuation as he intended it to be interpreted, then the punctuation is useless, or even misleading; and unless all writers use the same system, obviously all readers of any author, if he has many, will not understand his punctuation.

Punctuation, standardized and developed by printers, belongs to writing; we obviously cannot punctuate our speech. Yet some commentators on the subject seem to assume that we do, and some interrelation does of course exist between pauses in speech and punctuation in writing. Yet the two are not the same, and the blind are leading the blind whenever advice is given to "put a comma where you would pause in speaking." Consider the following expression: *The tall, magnificent building,* which is punctuated correctly. Read it correctly and a pause indeed occurs after *tall,* as it does in the expression *The tall red brick building,* which is also punctuated correctly. But in the first form, a pause at least as prolonged as that after *tall* occurs after *magnificent,* and the function of the comma BEFORE *magnificent* is, insofar as speech is at all related to writing, to create the pause AFTER *magnificent.* So much for punctuating to signal pauses.

Punctuation has little relation to elocutionary performance or any oral reading. Such relation as it does have springs from the fact that punctuation is grammatical, and that pauses in speech, which by no means occur regularly only where the punctuation is, do nevertheless constitute a principal means of signaling grammatical structure in speech. But we are concerned with writing, to be seen with the eye and not heard with the ear, and only in writing is punctuation involved. In written English, when positioning of words and such inflection as the language retains will not demonstrate grammatical relationships, punctuation frequently will, and that is its function.

This statement is not to be interpreted, let us hasten to add, as signifying that a muddled arrangement of words can be made intelligible by insertion of punctuation. Punctuation is in no sense a last resort for the writer who finds his own writing confusing. He cannot hope by inserting punctuation to avoid confusing his reader with what he himself finds confusing. Punctuation takes over where the best possible choice and arrangement of words has been achieved, but it is not a task to be performed after the writing is done. It is an aspect of writing, and should be carried on simultaneously with writing. An intelligent writer thinks grammatically. Just as he spells words as he writes, not afterward, so he punctuates in conformity to his arrangement of his words. His punctuation is part of his thinking and writing, and he uses it to signal to his reader the grammatical constructions he is using. Modern punctuation, reduced though it is from former practice, can signal grammatical stages of thought with great accuracy.

Before we turn to explanation of the prevailing system of punctuation, a word should be said again concerning its conventionality. It is a system of signals of grammatical structure, of the actual stages in the thought of the writer, an important aspect of the communication between author and reader. The signals must be interpreted by the reader just as they were intended by the author. Any deviation from such interpretation will at least temporarily, and perhaps permanently, impair communication between writer and reader. Hence punctuation must be a well-established convention of the literate society using the language. It must be part of a generally recognized mode of communication, a part of the written language itself.

It is thus a device of communication, and though it has its actually undeviating rules or principles, it is also one of the aspects of written English by means of which the writer communicates with the reader. Hence, though both writer and reader must understand the principles in the same way, the writer utilizes those principles to convey *his* meaning. When he punctuates he must punctuate by rule, but often he must exercise discretion, weighing his precise meaning against the significance of the rule, in deciding whether or not to punctuate. He is transmitting *his* thought, and he better than anyone else knows what his thought is. His precise meaning will not be conveyed if he gives his reader the wrong punctuation signal, and absence of punctuation is itself a signal, just as lack of illumination in a switchlight or on an instrument panel is a signal to the operator. It is of the utmost importance for the writer, then, to understand the principles of punctuation thoroughly and to practice them with all the discretion at his command.

We shall survey contemporary English punctuation as practiced in the United States (British punctuation, like British pronunciation, vocabulary, and spelling, not being altogether the same) by first presenting common uses of such punctuation marks as do not play any significant part in the internal punctuation of sentences. Later we shall consider separately the devices by which punctuation makes clear the grammatical relations within a sentence.

End Punctuation

That a sentence begins with a capital letter, and if it is declarative, ends with a period need hardly be pointed out. Practically the only other use of the period is after abbreviations, and this use is not universal. Roman numerals, the far-too-common initials of international and national organizations written in capitals and without spacing (UN, USSR, etc.), and chemical symbols, require no periods. Sentences that are not declarative sometimes fail to get proper punctuation at their end (? or !), but probably only through carelessness, not ignorance. In handwriting carelessness about insertion of periods can also be extremely annoying to a reader, especially in handwriting that does not distinguish well between capital and small letters, or where a capital at the beginning of a sentence would also appear elsewhere (a proper noun or *I*). In general, however, few literate persons have any trouble with punctuation at the end of a sentence.

Word Punctuation

Two punctuation marks (the hypen and the apostrophe) are used only in the punctuation of individual words and are actually still much influenced in their use by the spoken language.

One common use of the hyphen is between the syllables of a word at the end of a line when the following syllable or syllables must be carried to the next line. This use is affected by speech because syllable division is always determined by the pronunciation of a word, not by its etymological composition, and division must occur between the syllables. If one is in doubt about syllable division, the dictionary, of course, will always inform him. It is unwise to divide words unnecessarily; each line should contain either whole words (preferable) or a reasonable proportion of a divided word. An interesting problem arises, to which we know of no accepted solution, though some have been proposed, when a word that might anywhere be written with a hyphen, or might be so written by some people and not by others, gets divided at the hyphen because it comes at the end of a line. How is a writer to let any copyist or typesetter know whether he does or does not want the hyphen retained elsewhere than at the end of a line?

The other common use of the hyphen is in compound words, and it is a troublesome matter indeed. The trouble arises chiefly from the shifting of accent from one element of the possible compound to the other, and the accompanying slight pause or absence of it after the first element, that occurs in speech, so that an expression may be sensed by a speaker as two words, as a hyphenated word, or as a single word. Actually such expressions commonly go through this cycle of change. *Rail road* (a road of rails) was originally two words. Then came *rail-road*, and finally we have only *railroad*. Two words that only fairly recently thus became one flesh are *weekend* and *textbook*. One of the present writers recalls some years ago having felt serious qualms about writing *nonetheless*, but now it and *insofar* are common. To hyphenate or not to hyphenate, to write one word or two, is many times the question, and no unequivocal answer can be found until the evolution of the language supplies one, as it always will, eventually. But meanwhile we live and write in the present. The dictionary will often help, but one need not be slavishly bound by it. Adjectives, especially, are commonly hyphenated with no sanction but the writer's sense of propriety.

The best guide to this otherwise unsanctioned use is to remember the literal meaning of the word "hyphen," *under one* or *taken in one piece*. The hyphen thus binds together individual words to give them a single meaning. Adjectives before a noun often require the hyphen to prevent their being understood individually or to signal the logical impossibility of their being so understood, for sometimes hyphenated adjectives are not even composed of adjectives (like *make-believe*). Even adverbs that precede adjectives or participles used attributively may need to be bound to the adjectives or participles by a hyphen, especially when the adverb is a word that may also function as an adjective (notably *well*, as in *well-made*). But like other good things, unconventional hyphenation should not be overdone, for bizarre concatenations may delay or puzzle the reader just as would any other coined word.

Compounds, like other words, should be readily recognizable to the readers for whom they are intended.

When two compound words whose second element is the same have their unlike first elements linked by a conjunction and their common second element expressed only after the conjunction, a hyphen is used after both first elements *(The two- and three-story buildings)*.

THE APOSTROPHE

The apostrophe also has two principal uses. Its original use was to signal the omission of letters from a word, to fill the gap. This is speech-connected because of the common use of the apostrophe to mark elisions that are a regular feature of speech, but it is not a use of the apostrophe of such interest to expository writers as the other common one. This, of course, is in possessives (a use not developed until late in the seventeenth century under the misconception that the historical -*s* ending of possessives was a contraction of *his*, the form *Charles his hat* having been used under the same misconception earlier in the century).

For this use of the apostrophe the usual elaborate array of rules can be greatly simplified. If the writer, without regard to whether a word is singular or plural, will simply add an apostrophe when he wishes to make the word possessive provided it ends in an *s* or *z* sound, and still without regard to whether the word is singular or plural, add both the apostrophe and a following *s* provided the word does not end in an *s* or *z* sound, he has then only to consider whether the resulting possessive in the first instance is pronounceable without an additional *s* or *z* sound. If it is not, he should add another *s* after the apostrophe. (Of course, even in applying this simple rule, the writer must consider the form of the word *before* it was made possessive, whether it *then* did or did not end in an *s* or *z* sound.) Except for the possessive pronouns *his, hers, its, ours, yours, theirs,* the apostrophe should always appear in possessives. *(It's,* the elided form of *it is,* should be rigorously distinguished from *its,* the possessive pronoun.) As a sign of plurals, the apostrophe appears before the *s* only to pluralize figures, letters, symbols, and words referred to out of context as words, and even this use is waning. Adjectives ending in *s,* where no possession is involved, should not be confused with possessives *(The Dickens Society; a teachers college).*

QUOTATIONS

Three marks are used primarily with direct quotations: quotation marks, an ellipsis, and square brackets. Rather ironically, of these three marks quotation marks have the most use extraneous to quotations. They are used to distinguish a title within a larger publication, such as a chapter in a book or an article in a periodical or an encyclopedia, from the title of the whole work, which is put in italics. They are used to enclose terms felt to be somehow out of context, such as words referred to as words, colloquialisms in formal discourse, coined words, technical, trade, or shop jargon not expected to be familiar to the reader. In all but the first of these uses their significance is pretty well expressed in the phrase "as is said," or colloquially, "as they say."

Their primary use, as their name implies, is to enclose direct quotations, and when quotations are not signaled by indentation and change of type format, quotation marks must always be used. Only quoted material should appear between them, so that unless brackets are used (as explained below), at the beginning of any interruption of the quotation the quotation marks should be closed, and they should be opened again where the quotation is resumed. For a quotation within a quotation single quotation marks are used. (Our American practice thus reverses the British one of single marks generally used and double ones within them.) When a quotation contains more than one paragraph, the quotation marks are repeated at the beginning of each paragraph, but not closed until the end of the quotation. As to the conjunction of quotation marks with other punctuation marks at the end of a quotation, our American practice (again not the British) is always to place a period or comma within the quotation marks, and to treat all other punctuation marks in accordance with their significance, placing them within the quotation marks if they belong to the quotation and outside the marks if they belong to the sentence as a whole.

Square brackets ([]) are used almost exclusively for one purpose: to insert into a quotation remarks of the quoter's own without otherwise interrupting the quotation. With due notice by means of brackets one may insert anything he pleases into a quotation. For the opposite purpose of omitting from a quotation parts unrelated to one's thought an ellipsis mark of three dots (. . .) is used. Honesty, of course, demands that the person quoted be in no way misrepresented by partial quotation. If a period belonging to the quotation comes into conjunction with an ellipsis, then of course three plus one equals four (. . . .).

INTERNAL PUNCTUATION OF SENTENCES

Complicated as the rules for internal punctuation of the sentence may often appear, the grammatical structures that are regularly signaled by such punctuation are actually only four: compounds, preliminary modifiers, series, and interruptions. The punctuation marks required for internal punctuation are the comma (,), semicolon (;), colon (:), dash (−), and parentheses, but we shall organize our discussion in this final section around each of the four grammatical structures that requires punctuation, alluding to the punctuation marks themselves only as the grammatical situation calls for their use.

COMPOUNDS

A compound sentence (made up of two or more potential simple sentences) usually requires punctuation between its independent clauses. Omission of this punctuation is sometimes preferable when only two short clauses are involved, especially if they have related subjects, if a preliminary modifier refers to both of them, or if they otherwise make closely related assertions. Such situations are relatively rare, however, and compound sentences generally require punctuation.

The rule for their punctuation is simple: If the clauses are connected by a simple co-ordinating conjunction (*and, but,** for, or,* or *nor*), a comma should be used before the conjunction; otherwise either a semicolon or a colon should be used. With no connec-

---

* Because of its adversative meaning, *but* requires punctuation before it more frequently than the other co-ordinating conjunctions.

tive, then, or with any connective other than the five words listed, a comma will not suffice, but a semicolon should generally be used.

The colon, which is always nowadays a mark of anticipation, meaning *Note what is to follow*, should be used in those somewhat rare instances in which, with no connective involved, what follows the first independent clause is explanatory or elucidatory of that first clause. The colon may be used in this way when what follows the completed first clause is not itself an independent clause but a list or series or other elucidation of the completed clause, having the effect of supplementing the completed clause without being any structural part of it. This is the only present use of the colon within sentences.

The semicolon may sometimes be required before a simple conjunction in a compound sentence because so many commas have occurred in the long independent clauses that a comma is not adequate to signal the main grammatical distinction of the independent clauses in the sentence. When a compound sentence becomes thus choked with commas, however, one should question whether revision is not a better means of clarification than is punctuation, or whether minimizing of other punctuation (as explained at the end of the discussion of the *a, b,* and *c* series below) may not offer a better solution than resorting to semicolons.

Sometimes, not only compound sentences, but compound predicates require punctuation. This requirement develops when the second part of the predicate is fairly long and is felt to make an assertion quite disparate from the first part of it. Even then a comma should suffice.

Generally the relation to each other of compound

subordinate clauses that are not restrictive is made clearer if they are separated by a comma — *If the mixture has thoroughly coagulated, and if all possibility of later liquefaction has passed, then we may* . . . or *The experimenter should be certain that the mixture has thoroughly coagulated, and that all possibility of later liquefaction has passed.*

PRELIMINARY ADVERBIAL MODIFIERS

Preliminary or introductory adverbial modifiers often need to be separated by a comma from the main clause that follows them. These may begin the sentence or occur elsewhere within it before the main clause they modify. If such preliminary modifiers are clauses, they generally require the comma after them. Exceptions do arise when the preliminary clause is exceedingly short, has the same subject as its main clause, or is felt to restrict its referent in the following main clause. Preliminary elliptical clauses or infinitives or participial phrases require the same treatment as full preliminary clauses, and are usually set off by a comma. Preliminary prepositional phrases do not so frequently require this punctuation, and need be set off only if they are quite long, are strongly nonrestrictive, or require emphasis. Individual preliminary adverbs are set off only when they are strongly nonrestrictive or require emphasis, as they quite commonly are or do.

SERIES

Series requiring punctuation are of two kinds: the *a, b,* and *c* type and parallel adjectives or adverbs. The conventional manner of punctuating the *a, b,* and *c* series is exactly that represented in the statement of it — with a comma to separate each of the parallel elements in the series from those before and after it. The series may, of course, be composed of more than three such parallel elements, and the elements may be single words, phrases, or clauses, any or all with modifiers. The conjunction need not be *and*. Parallelism is the essential feature of a series, and therefore its elements, whatever their grammatical structure, must be of the same structure.

In the modern enthusiasm over "loose," or economical, punctuation, some writers and publishers have advocated and practiced omission of the comma before the conjunction in this series. In our opinion this practice carries economy of punctuation dangerously far. Often the last two elements of the series have in their meaning a natural affinity for each other that results in uncertainty, when the comma is omitted between them, as to whether they are to be accepted in the series as one or two elements. Consider the following sentence: *The officers shall be a president, vice-president, secretary and treasurer.* With no comma after *secretary,* how many officers are alluded to, three or four? This ambiguity arises rather commonly and would in itself be a sufficient reason to practice use of the comma before the conjunction, just as between other elements of the *a, b,* and *c* series. But an even greater necessity for the comma in this position arises from its function to signal the termination of the series. Consider, thus punctuated, a sentence that occurs earlier in this chapter (p. 151): *Roman numerals, the far-too-common initials of international and national organizations written in capitals and without spacing (UN, USSR, etc.) and chemical symbols require no periods.* The reader probably did not here apprehend the meaning of the sentence at first glance. The reason is that the close of the *a, b,* and *c* series is not signaled.

The sentence raises another interesting point in the punctuation of the *a, b,* and *c* series as subject of a verb. It appears in this book thus: *Roman numerals, the far-too-common initials of international and national organizations written in capitals and without spacing (UN, USSR, etc.), and chemical symbols, require no periods.* Not only were commas inserted to separate each of the elements of the series from those before and after, but a comma was inserted after the series and before the verb of which the whole series is the subject, because it was felt that here even separation of each element in the series from the others did not adequately signal the termination of the series. The word *all* might have been inserted after the last comma, but then the comma surely would have been essential. The comma alone can adequately close the series and is needed for this purpose. But notice in the illustrative sentence as last quoted how ridiculously confusing it would be to retain the comma before *require* and remove the comma before *and.* For these reasons, then, it is our conviction that all elements in an *a, b,* and *c* series require separation from each other by commas. An important function of the comma before the conjunction is to signal the end of the series. Yet when the elements of such a series are complicated and are used as the compound subject of a single verb, the termination of the series is not always adequately signaled by punctuation of the series alone and must be further signaled by a comma at the end of the series.

Very occasionally indeed, it may become necessary to separate the elements of an *a, b,* and *c* series from each other by semicolons because some or all of the elements contain so many commas that commas do not seem to provide adequate separation of the series elements from one another. The practice is best reserved, however, for series in which the elements are themselves independent clauses, when what is actually involved is punctuation of compounds rather than of series. Certainly clausal or phrasal modifiers should never be separated from their main clauses by semicolons. Semicolons may perhaps be used to separate complicated elements of a series that ends a sentence, but overloading of the sentence should always be suspected when this necessity arises anywhere in it.

A better solution for multiplicity of commas than resorting to semicolons is to reduce the number of commas in the sentence by dropping minor punctuation. In a long and complicated sentence, reduced punctuation of its elements may be safely practiced. Adjectives that are actually in parallel series (discussed just below) or modifiers of various sorts, even phrasal and clausal modifiers (but not usually nonrestrictive relative clauses), may be left unpunctuated to signal themselves without punctuation when commas must be saved to mark major grammatical elements in a complicated sentence. No confusion need arise from judicious application of this principle, but it is, of course, the writer's responsibility to be sure that none does. Since series of independent clauses are compound sentences, the necessity for semicolons in them may often be avoided by this same economy in minor punctuation.

An advisable economy to be practiced at all possible times is the omission of punctuation immediately after conjunctions, especially co-ordinating conjunctions. An interruption that begins at this point is usually signaled adequately by the conjunction and any punctuation before it. Punctuation occurring before the conjunction because of compounding or series will usually perform satisfactorily the additional duty of signaling a sequent interruption, and if punctuation is not otherwise required before the conjunction, it is in our opinion usually best to consider that the interruption begins with the conjunction and place before the conjunction any punctuation required by the interruption. One thus avoids illogically separating by punctuation the conjunction, a word whose function is to introduce additional thought, from what it introduces. Especially illogical is the complete isolation of the conjunction by means of punctuation both immediately before and immediately after it.

The series of parallel adjectives or adverbs offers difficulty chiefly in determining whether the adjectives or adverbs involved actually are parallel, whether a series actually exists. Compare (slightly altered) the phrases alluded to earlier in this chapter: *The red brick building* and *The tall, handsome building.* The distinction here would be signaled in speech, but the principal difference in timing would occur in a distinct pause AFTER *handsome,* where a comma should by no means be placed. A logical distinction can also be made: parallel adjectives or adverbs are all felt to affect their referent with the same force, those nearer to the referent being no more closely associated with it than those more distant. In the example above, *tall* and *handsome* are parallel because neither tallness nor handsomeness is felt to be a more important attribute of the building than the other. But in the other expression, the building is felt to be essentially brick, and both building and brick to be red. Inversion of the elements sometimes helps to make the distinction. *The handsome, tall building* is acceptable; no significant change has resulted from the inversion. *The brick red building* seems to require a hyphen between *brick* and *red* instead of a comma, for now the building is no longer constructed of brick, but is brick-red in color. *Brick* cannot be moved from its proximity to *building* without obvious change in the meaning of the expression because *brick* and *red* are not here parallel. Parallelism of modifiers should be recognized and signaled by insertion of commas between them, but if one is at all doubtful whether parallelism exists, whether he is actually dealing with a series, it is safer to omit commas rather than insert them. Such a series may, of course, be composed of more than two elements, and when more than two adjectives or adverbs are in sequence, some but not all of them may be parallel, as in *The tall, powerful old man.*

INTERRUPTION

Interruption probably accounts for well over fifty percent of our internal sentence punctuation. Here are grouped those constructions that are commonly referred to as either nonrestrictive or parenthetic, for both are interruptions of the natural flow of thought, though they are essential interruptions that contribute much to the flexibility of language and the subtle profusion of thought it can express. Simply to remark that any interruption of thought requires punctuation before and after it (unless it reaches the period at the end of the sentence), to separate it from the flow of thought interrupted, is to solve the whole problem in one sweeping generalization. But generalizations are not usually helpful to one who is not acquainted with the details generalized. On the other hand, the multiplicity of interruptions that both beset and enrich the English sentence defy classification. Only samples of the detail will be dealt with here.

The nonrestrictive relative clause is a familiar form of interruption. A restrictive relative clause limits or identifies (in short, restricts) its referent, and being thus an essential element of the thought of the sentence, it should not be separated from the main idea of the sentence by any punctuation. (Example: *The man who just entered the room is our speaker. The man* is identified by *who just entered the room.*) A nonrestrictive clause by definition does no such restricting (identifying or limiting). Although such a clause cannot always literally be omitted without damage to the main clause (because sometimes it contains an element essential to the main thought, such as a referent for a pronoun in the main clause or a complete verb that is alluded to only in clipped form in the main clause), as a modifier it contributes nothing of significance to the main clause. (Example: *Dr. William Smith, who just entered the room, is our speaker. Dr. William Smith* is presumably well identified by his name, and *who just entered the room* merely calls incidental attention to his entrance.) An example of a nonrestrictive clause that cannot literally be omitted from the sentence without disrupting it is the following: *The courthouse, which stands in the village square, dominates it.*

But it should be clearly understood that a writer does not punctuate or refrain from punctuating a relative clause because the clause dictates its own punctuation. The reverse is often true: he punctuates or declines to punctuate in order that his reader may know what his sentence means. *The men who came here yesterday are waiting to see you* has one meaning unpunctuated and a distinctly different meaning if punctuated. The writer must learn to distinguish between restrictive and nonrestrictive clauses and practice the distinction in his punctuation, which, as has been said, is an essential aspect of his communication.

OTHER NONRESTRICTION

But relative clauses are only one type of modifier, and any modifier may be nonrestrictive. Adverbial clauses that are preliminary, we saw above, are generally set off by a comma, but adverbial clauses that follow their referent are set off in accordance with whether they are restrictive or nonrestrictive (compare *I came when I could get away* with *I came at the end of the day, when I was able to get away*). Phrases of all sorts and single-word modifiers may also be nonrestrictive and require separation with commas from the rest of the sentence. The principle is of wide application. An adjective following a referent is often nonrestrictive, and in general, modifiers out of normal position become nonrestrictive, for punctuation then is needed to indicate the thought relationship that their position does not convey, as well as to prevent establishing false thought relationships. Thus punctuation confirms grammatical structure. But nonrestriction is not, conversely, dependent upon misplacement. It is often, as in relative clauses, inherent in the character of the modifier itself, and punctuation must then perform a task of guiding the reader's thought that no positioning could accomplish.

PARENTHESIS

Parenthesis is not always distinguishable from non-restriction, but fortunately, since both are interruptions, the distinction is not significant. The general distinction is that parenthetic expressions need not be modifiers. They are punctuated, however, just like nonrestrictive modifiers. Appositives may or may not be parenthetic in accordance with their felt closeness to their referent, actually their restriction or non-restriction of it. If they result from eliding a relative clause, however, whatever the nature of the clause, they are sure to be parenthetic. Conjunctive adverbs used to bridge the thought between the sentence in which they occur and that of the sentence or sentences that precede it (such as *however, moreover, furthermore, then, nevertheless,* and the like) are, wherever placed in the sentence, parenthetic. But the possibilities of interruptions are legion, as numerous as the often not unfruitful interruptions in our busy lives. Some of those that might prove troublesome have been mentioned. The writer will in general recognize them, and must utilize punctuation to apprise the reader of them as clearly yet discreetly as possible, for they and their punctuation are both an essential part of writer-reader communication.

Commas usually suffice to set off interruptions, and stronger marks should be resorted to only when needed. These stronger marks are dashes and parentheses, and to enclose interruptions is their only function. Whenever the comma is felt to be an insufficient signal of the force of the interruption, dashes or parentheses are used. Like commas used for this purpose, they are used in pairs to enclose the interruption from both ends, unless the interruption terminates with the sentence, and even then the parentheses, not dashes, are closed before the end punctuation of the sentence. A comma coinciding with a dash should precede it. Parentheses sometimes enclose one or more complete sentences, and then the closing parenthesis is not followed by any punctuation. No sharp distinction is made in a choice between dashes and parentheses, but the use of parentheses instead of dashes is increasing, probably because of former overuse of dashes, although the more clearly embracing appearance of parentheses may seem to recommend them for the clean break of a sharp interruption. Where the two are used in combination, parentheses are rated the stronger mark, so that dashes are used within parentheses, not parentheses within dashes. In this use, the closing dash should be omitted if the interruption it was designed to enclose reaches the final parenthesis.

AT SENTENCE END
> Period
> Question mark
> Exclamation point

WITHIN WORDS
> Hyphen
> Apostrophe

OF QUOTATIONS
> Quotation marks
> Square brackets
> Ellipsis

WITHIN SENTENCES
> *Comma* separates:
>> Most preliminary modifiers
>> Independent clauses connected by *and, but, for, or, nor,* and sometimes a compound predicate so connected
>> Items in a series
>> Nonrestrictive or parenthetic interruptions
>
> *Semicolon* separates independent clauses not connected by *and, but, for, or,* or *nor,* and occasionally replaces a comma in a compound sentence or a series when many commas occur in its elements
>
> *Colon* has only anticipatory use after an independent clause to signal the explanatory significance of what follows
>
> *Dashes and parentheses* are resorted to when nonrestriction or parenthesis creates a particularly abrupt interruption

IX

TROUBLESHOOTING

After a writer has composed a work, he faces the challenge of finding and smoothing as many of the remaining rough spots as he can. This chapter contains suggestions for isolating the places that need improvement.

An author, of course, always has difficulty approaching his work in the way a reader will. Even laying the work aside for considerable time will never quite erase the writer's memory of what it was intended to say. Criticizing one's own work is like trying to hear one's own voice without the aid of a tape recorder. The originator is too close to the source and perceives it through pathways that are unavailable to others and cannot be effectively blocked for him. Imagination and open-mindedness are the only effective tools for combatting these problems.

FINDING ROUGH SPOTS

The standard tactics are laying the work aside for a time and seeking the opinions of others. Laying the material aside is an excellent tactic, but allowing it to "cool" sufficiently to make much difference on rereading is not always practical.

Seeking the opinions of others can be helpful, but the usual difficulty is that others do not have the same interests as the writer, and unless they are professional editors, they may fail to examine the work carefully.

They have probably also found that their detailed suggestions are frequently ignored. To some extent, it is not possible for another person to trim up a paper without rewriting it in his own personal style. That is, the criticisms of another may concentrate unduly on spots where his style would differ most from the author's, not where a general reader would necessarily have the greatest difficulties.

An author must therefore rely upon his own judgement in the end. This does not mean that the reactions of others are valueless. They can be most helpful when help is requested in the proper way. Instead of asking for general suggestions, ask for reactions. That is, ask the reader to note where he had trouble understanding the material, where he had to read the passages twice, which sections seemed clearest, which parts he would eliminate if someone were to insist that the paper be shortened. One may thus obtain his reactions as a reader rather than as another writer.

An author is fortunate if he can call on the services of a professional editor. Do not make the mistake of assuming that, just because an editor may be unable to follow the technical arguments, he cannot recognize unclear English when he sees it. A good editor has a professional love for language and need not understand the detailed message to recognize unclear or vague passages. Language is language, and illogical juxtapositions of words, vague phrases, or contorted grammar are not likely to convey a clear explanation of anything, however abstruse the subject matter. To obtain the most benefit from editorial services, the writer must, however, do his share. The editor is the first completely unprepared reader, and as such, can point out many rough spots, but he usually cannot devise an adequate cure without the writer's help, because he does not have the necessary technical knowledge. His role is that of a critic, and he will try to be constructive, but he needs help, not resistance.

A few devices can aid the writer himself to imagine the reactions of a reader:

Try reading very rapidly. Exaggerated speed compensates, to some extent, for the author's knowledge of what is coming next. Regard with suspicion any passage where the pace must be slowed or where any words or sentences must be retraced, even briefly. Such delays, to a mind that knows the message, almost certainly indicate a corresponding, more serious difficulty for at least some readers.

Try to "read in a monotone." It is difficult for a writer to forget the pattern of stress that he had in mind as he composed. Any such stress, of course, no longer exists in print. Consequently, in rereading, it is important not to declaim the words mentally, in imitation of an orator. An absolutely even monotone is closer to the effect that a sight-reader will receive from the printed words. If a stress-pattern is needed to carry the meaning, or merely to clarify the grammar, many readers will miss the intended meaning or have trouble grasping the grammatical sense.

Consciously try to misread. That is, search deliberately for other ways, natural or unnatural, of interpreting the same words. What is unnatural to one reader may seem natural to another. In particular, try altering the "natural" pattern of stress to see whether other meanings emerge. If the meaning of a sentence can be significantly altered in this way, it will be misunderstood by some readers and will confuse or delay others.

Diagnosis

After the writer has located a sentence that requires further revision, he must decide upon the source of the difficulty and devise a cure. If the source is not immediately obvious, the following questions may help to locate the trouble.

GRAMMATICAL GUIDANCE

— Which pairs of words are grammatically related? Are they sufficiently close to one another? Does the reader have to hold any "grammatical loose ends" in mind?

— Which clause contains the most important thought? Is it the main grammatical clause?

— What is the logical subject of the main thought? Is it the main grammatical subject?

— Can interrupting clauses or phrases be moved ahead of the main subject or after the main clause?

— Can modifiers be shortened?

— Would active voice be smoother than passive voice?

— Should an elliptical clause be expanded into full form?

— Might the sentence be broken into two or more sentences? Or should it be combined with another sentence?

CLARITY OF STYLE, EXPLICITNESS

— Is the main verb serving a main purpose?

— What necessary purpose does each word have?

— Can modifiers be eliminated by a more precise

choice for the word they modify? (Should a vague noun be replaced by the noun-form of one of the modifiers, for example?)

— Can modifiers be shortened? (Phrases to simple adjectives or adverbs, clauses to phrases or appositives? Can some prepositions or relative pronouns be eliminated?)

— Should "which" be changed to "that" to indicate that a clause is vital to the meaning?

— Are "when," "where," "while" properly used?

— Does each preposition express accurately the relation between its object and the remainder of the sentence?

Beware of insertions. Revision, of course, necessarily entails insertions as well as deletions, but hasty insertions are a frequent source of grammatical interruptions, and insertion of entire sentences sometimes interrupts continuity of thought. Therefore be wary of insertions, and check thoroughly to see that the grammar remains smooth and that any necessary transitional ideas have been supplied along with those inserted.

Again recall that if a sentence appears to need an extra modifier or a change in wording to reinforce an implication, then it should probably be replaced by a paragraph. If the implication is important to the writer, he should give it an explicit form that the reader will not miss.

Danger Signals

Another device for locating some of the reader's difficulties is to check on the use of a number of words and phrases that, while entirely proper English, are frequently the basis for awkward or unnecessary constructions. We do not, of course, suggest or imply in any way that the words and phrases listed below should be proscribed. Each has its value, but each also has common misuses, and a check on the use of these words will often uncover certain types of ineptitudes.

There are . . . X . . . which . . .

Unless the existence of X is more important than its properties, this should be replaced by: *X . . . , Many X . . .* , or the like, which allow the main clause to express the properties of X.

. . . so that . . .

Often *X so that Y* is written when the meaning is *Because X, Y;* or *Y, because X,* both of which properly express the primary thought in the main clause.

. . . has as . . .

Relations such as

$$X \text{ has as } Y, Z$$

or $\qquad X \text{ has } Z \text{ as } Y$

are much clearer in the form

The Y of X is Z.

For example, *The main source of power for the space craft is an array of solar batteries* is much smoother than *The space craft has as its main source of power an array of solar batteries.* When the items are more complicated than these, the greater readability of the direct form is correspondingly more striking.

However, Also, and the like

These words as conjunctive adverbs introducing a sentence often usurp the emphasis that properly belongs to the subject or another sentence element. As lead-off words they may also overemphasize the closeness of their sentence to the preceding one and obscure sentence individuality. It is frequently better to insert them elsewhere. For desired strong initial contrast, the less equivocal *But* can substitute for *However*.

Weak or Vacuous Words (useful, important, interesting . . .)

Such words have proper English meanings, but they are frequently inserted to fill a grammatical hiatus or to make the sentence appear to say something more generally significant than it really does. In such uses, these words merely fill space and complicate the grammar without conveying any information. *The importance of this relationship to the present study is its usefulness as . . .*

. . . sufficiently . . . that . . .

This construction is becoming common, but it still jars many readers. The meaning is often, *sufficiently . . . to . . .* or *sufficiently . . . for . . .* If these cannot be used, *sufficiently . . . so that . . .* would be smoother. Sometimes, *so . . . (adjective or adverb) . . . that . . . (so red that . . .* for example) is more effective.

STRINGS OF SMALL WORDS

Strings of monosyllables often indicate an involved grammatical structure, for example, a compound verb interrupted by an adverbial phrase, or the like. If each monosyllable is vital to the sense, the reader may be led astray by missing one.

of STRINGS (A of B of C of D . . .)

Usually some of the phrases can be replaced by adjectives, with great increase in clarity.

STRINGS OF NOUNS (not a list)

All but one of the nouns in such a string is used as an adjective. Must the reader readjust his interpretation too often before discovering the true noun?

OVERUSE OF HYPHENS

Occasionally, a writer attempts to improve readability by inserting a hyphen between two words that are very long or seldom closely associated. Unwieldy or unnatural hyphenated compounds will only delay the reader in the same way that a bizarre or nonstandard word would delay him.

. . . *such* . . . (as pronoun)

This pronoun is relatively unfamiliar and not as readily recognized as other pronouns. Repeat the noun or name the concept for which it stands unless the context is particularly brief and clear.

ABBREVIATIONS

Unless an abbreviation is absolutely required to help the reader (not the writer!), it should be replaced by the full words for which it stands. The reader can grasp them faster!

DOUBLE NEGATIVES (*not unlike*, etc.)

In short sentences double negatives can be clear, but as a sentence is lengthened, they first tend to sound stilted, and eventually become difficult to follow.

latter, former, the second, the last, etc.

It is a rare reader who can recognize the references of these words without glancing back to check the previous arrangement. A brief descriptive, or at least suggestive, name should be used instead whenever possible.

. . . due to . . .

Due to is adjectival, not adverbial, and must modify a noun (or equivalent), never a verb or entire thought. *Death due to drowning,* not *He died due to drowning.* Also not, *This is complicated due to . . .*

. . . phenomenon . . .

Frequently *the phenomena of* X means simply X.

. . . the use of . . .

In many constructions, these words are vacuous. For example, X *was avoided by the use of* Y often means merely Y *avoided* X or X *was avoided by* Y.

POINTLESS GENERALITIES

Frequently a main substantive is vacuous. Examples:
>   *the problem of computing*
>   *the concept of justice*
>   *the subject of mathematics*
>   *the development of history*
>   *the function of . . .*
>   *the use of . . .*
>   *the phenomenon of . . .*

. . . from the point of view of . . .

This long phrase is often quite unnecessary. If it expresses any significant modification, a simple adverb or a shorter phrase *(with regard to,* for example) will usually suffice.

affect, effect

In their usual meanings, *effect* is the noun, and *affect* is the verb (to have an effect upon).

(In the rare use, *effect* as a verb means to cause or to accomplish — to bring into effect. In still rarer use, *affect* as a noun means a disposition or emotion.)

. . . effects . . . (as a noun)

This noun is a general, vague word, and its use, particularly with a modifier, often indicates vagueness or unnecessary complexity:

> *damaging effects (damage)*
> *the net effect is . . . (effectively . . .)*
> *the effects of X are . . . (X produces . . .*
> *or X entails . . .)*

. . . results . . .

Results is also a general word and therefore sometimes indicates vagueness or complexity:

> *The results of this investigation are . . .*
> *(This investigation shows . . .*
> *demonstrates . . .*
> *suggests . . .)*

. . . in that . . .

This phrase is a perfectly correct substitute for *because,* but it is unfortunately formed from two very common words, which usually have entirely different functions *(in that box).* *Because* or *since* is usually a much less ambiguous signal for a dependent, logically supporting clause.

. . . have come to occupy a place of . . .

The meaning is merely, *are* or *have become* or *act as.*

. . . has the function of . . .

This phrase is vacuous: *. . . has the function of ensuring . . .* means simply, *. . . ensures . . .*

. . . by virtue of . . .

The meaning is *by* or *through.*

. . . in the case of (or *where*) *. . .*

The meaning is usually *when* or *with.*

EXCESSIVE PUNCTUATION

When a sentence requires an excessive number of commas or entails dashes within parentheses, it is often clumsily constructed. Can the reader easily pair the commas and perceive the structure? Usually, re-arranging or splitting the sentence into several sentences is the safest course.

The above admonitions, and indeed all this small book, are meant to be only suggestive. They are certainly not exhaustive. An attentive writer will find other ways to "help the reader." A good writer is a good reader, constantly aware of effective and ineffective expression in the work of others. Direct imitation of other writers may have value as an exercise in self-improvement, but it is not the road to permanent facility in expression. One must develop his own style, for his expression is a reflection of his own unique mind. One thinks the way he writes and writes the way he thinks. The objective is to think and write better, though not exactly like anyone else. Even Shakespeare wrote better and less imitatively from play to play. The danger is in getting into a rut of habitual phraseology. We all develop characteristic habits of expression, many of them not as effective as they might be. Studying the felicitous expression of others and analyzing their clumsy ineptitudes will brighten our own style and cure our bad habits. Only a good reader can be a good writer, for if in communication one is content with poor reception, he will never make much attempt to improve his own transmission. Ralph Waldo Emerson said of the really great writers, "... if you can hear what these patriarchs say, surely you can reply to them in the same pitch of voice; for the ear and the tongue are two organs of one nature."

Yet perfection in expression, as in all human endeavor, is unattainable. No matter how carefully an author writes, then revises and re-revises, and finally scans proof sheets, errors that, if he is sensitive to such things, he will later regret will probably linger in his work. Even John Keats in his exquisite *The Eve of St. Agnes* found it necessary to clarify an ambiguous word in the lines, "her maiden eyes divine,/Fixed on the floor, saw many a sweeping train/Pass by": "I do not use *train* for *concourse of passers-by*, but for *skirts* sweeping along the floor." Surely, as Keats must have later recognized, the ambiguity is unfortunate. And Byron sometimes became downright ungrammatical in establishing a rhyme, as in his passionate invocation of the ocean at the end of *Childe Harold's Pilgrimage:* "And dashest him again to earth: — there let him lay." These authors and many others have achieved fame without achieving perfection. Nevertheless, the objective is to minimize ineptitudes by unremitting attempts to eliminate them. By taking thought a man may add to his stature, but never to the extent of becoming an impregnable tower of perfection.

APPENDIX

AUTHOR AND PRINTER

Printing from metallic type is inherently more complex than typewriting, and if an author understands some of the problems and methods of the printer, he can avoid unnecessary frustrations and ensure closer approximations to his wishes in the final product.

We cannot effectively discuss the many special requirements that are imposed by each individual technical journal, in order to ensure uniformity of the journal as a whole. Needless to say, such requests in regard to the style of references, footnotes, vector notation, and the like, should be honored, even when they entail retyping a manuscript that was originally prepared for another purpose. Otherwise, the author is forcing the editorial staff of the journal to do extra work that only he can do properly.

The purpose of this appendix will be to discuss principally book publishing. Except for the format conventions mentioned above, journal publishing differs primarily because the author has no control over page layout, type styles, or the typography of headings, and he receives only the first galley proofs. In other respects, the practices and problems are essentially the same, at least at the general level of our discussion.

First, it is helpful to realize that the publisher and the printer are two different people. In modern practice, they are often members of two completely independent firms. In either case, the publisher, after more or less consultation with the author, decides upon type styles and layout, edits the manuscript accordingly for the printer, and eventually supervises the distribution and sales of the book. He, of course, provides the capital funds to finance the venture. The printer, generally speaking, actually manufactures the book, although he or the publisher may, in practice, subcontract some of the purely mechanical operations to still more specialized firms.

Thus, it is clear that a manuscript will pass through many hands before any metallic type is set. Since both the publisher and the printer may have many specialized employees, at least as many as four people will read, and perhaps annotate, every page that the author submits. Accordingly, the author should:

— Use sturdy, white paper that will remain clean and smooth under repeated handling. Write only on one side.

— Typewrite all material that is to be printed, so that each letter will be clear and unmistakable to the typesetter. (Symbols not available on the typewriter must be carefully printed in ink and defined by a pencilled note — unless they have been very recently identified by an earlier note.)

— Leave wide margins and use double spacing to provide plenty of space for the publisher's notes to the printer. (Material to be set in small type can be single-spaced, but should be indented to leave a wider margin.)

Remember that even very high quality paper is cheap compared to the investment that the writer already has in the work, and compared to the labor that he must expend in preparing the final manuscript.

When one further considers the labor and trouble that can arise from unclear instructions, it manifestly behooves the writer to use as much good paper as necessary and to prepare it as carefully as he can.

Mathematical expressions require particular care because the typesetter can set only what he sees on the paper; he knows that his mathematical judgement is not reliable. Even roman characters should be identified if there can be any doubt about them. For example, the characters γ, r, v, V, ν are difficult to distinguish in the hand printing of many authors, and clarifying such matters may be even more important than identifying some Greek letters. Moreover, an untrained person does not "see" alinements that may be obvious to a mathematician. For this reason, subscripts and superscripts should be marked by carets and inverted carets respectively, and subscripts *to* superscripts should have a caret within the inverted caret, and so on. Although American practice traditionally calls for carets (with sharp corners), smooth arches or inverted arches (the British system) will serve equally well to guide the typesetter's eye along the various horizontal levels that the author desires in the final expression.

Mathematics unavoidably causes considerable trouble in setting metallic type. Type is carried on metal blocks of equal height, designed to be set in lines with smooth edges, fitting precisely against the line above and below, but mathematical notation evolves in day-to-day handwriting, where the size and location of the symbols can be varied at will. A clever typesetter, working by hand, can duplicate almost any mathematical expression, but this process can be extremely expensive compared to machine (keyboard) setting.

Type fonts used for mathematical works usually include complete sets of superscripts and subscripts, but all except the most common fractions must be built up from two rows of type with an intervening, hand-set horizontal line, unless they are written with a solidus ($/$). To set by machine as much mathematics as possible, most technical journals beseech authors to use negative exponents or the solidus. Similarly, because the "roof" on a square-root sign requires hand setting, most journals request fractional exponents. (Another solution, not often suggested, is to use an unroofed surd with parentheses, $\sqrt{(a^2-b^2)}$, which can also be set from a keyboard.)

A dot, caret, bar, or tilde above or below a letter cannot be properly set by machine unless the entire symbol (letter with dot, etc.) is available. The only other possibility is to insert an extra line, blank except for a period falling above the letter in the line below. Similarly, a superscript on a superscript (as in e^y where $y = x^2$) requires setting a single subscript (which would be "2" in the example) in the proper place on an otherwise blank, preceding line. Note that, to set the special line, the operator must know the positions of the symbols in the following, main line.

On the other hand, a subscript to a superscript can easily be set by using smaller type for the subscript. This possibility arises because, to allow a variety of line spacings, a given size of type face is manufactured on bodies (base blocks) of several heights, and all type sizes are alined with their bottom edges at the same height on a given body. Hence, with a given line spacing (a given body height), a smaller letter appears to be centered somewhat lower than a large letter. The superscript characters of a smaller type size therefore appear lower than the standard superscripts and can be used to subscript them. A similar but less satisfactory subscripting of subscripts can be achieved if a small alined letter is used for the main subscript and a small subscript for the sub-subscript. This scheme, however, works well only when both subscripts are lower case letters.

A universal cure for difficulties with subscripts and superscripts is a notation similar to the Dirac notation of quantum mechanics. Thus A_{ij} may be replaced by $[i|A|j]$ or $A(i,j)$. When the subscripts are sufficiently complicated, this may be the only way to preserve clarity.

Since all type will first be set in essentially one long, continuous column, footnotes need not be placed at the bottom of the manuscript pages, but may be typed in the middle of a page, separated from the main text by a pair of horizontal lines.

It is wise to number the manuscript pages in pencil to allow for last-minute insertions or revisions. The publisher should ideally receive sheets that are consecutively numbered with whole numbers (so that he can tell at a glance whether a page is missing), but some compromise is usually allowable. Added pages may be numbered "23a, 23b, . . ." but the preceding page ("23") must then carry the notation, "Pages 23a, 23b, . . . follow." Similarly, if pages are deleted, the page ahead of them should carry all the missing numbers as well as its own, for example, "27-29" if pages 28 and 29 have been deleted.

Corrections to the typescript, while never desirable, are allowable if they are clear and not too distracting for the typesetter, who cannot work at full speed if he must ponder the text or skip about on the page. Thus, corrections should be printed or typed between the lines of the text, not in the margin. They should never be written sideways in the margins, for this slows the typesetter by forcing him to turn the page. Likewise, long leader-arrows are likely to slow his work; a bulky insertion is best handled by crossing out text at the bottom (or top) of a page and typing the insertion together with this text on an additional page.

The fundamental principle behind all these remarks is simply that a manuscript should be a clear, complete set of instructions for setting metallic type. It is not a draft; it is a detailed directive for manufacturing a book. Thus, all loose ends should be tied down. Photographs or illustrations should be numbered on the back (with a *soft* pencil or crayon to avoid damage), and corresponding notations in the body of the manuscript should indicate where each one is to appear. Footnotes and references should be complete in all details, and any quotations should be carefully checked against their sources, if only for the author's own protection.

It is also the author's job to obtain legal permission to quote or reproduce copyrighted material. Most publishing contracts make the author liable for any copyright violations, and he must obtain his own protection in the form of written, duly signed permission from the copyright holder.

Publishers' attitudes toward editing the manuscript vary considerably. Although we have advocated in this book the forms that we consider preferable, tastes unquestionably differ, and no single set of practices can be defended as uniquely proper. In general, our advice to an author would be to accede to most of the editors' desires, reserving his right to specify what shall be published under his name for matters that are of utmost importance to him. A competent editor will seldom suggest changes that are really damaging, and if the author yields on the minutiae, his position will be that much stronger when he feels that something significant is at stake.

The publisher is usually quite willing to decide upon variations in type size and style (font) for subheadings and the like. With his experience, he can usually visualize better than the author what the final appearance will be. Nevertheless, if the author wishes, there is no objection to his using the standard underlining codes to indicate his preferences. (See the table printed at the end of this appendix.) In this connection, note that, to a typesetter, an underline does not mean "make this stand out," but rather it means "use italic type." Double underlining does not mean "make this *really* stand out"; it simply means "use small capitals."

Many journals request that vectors be marked with a wavy underline because this is the standard signal for boldface type.

Above all, be sure that the manuscript is in final form when it is submitted for typesetting. Once the metallic type has been assembled, alterations (except deletion or insertion of entire paragraphs) must be made partly or wholly by hand, an inherently inefficient, expensive process. Moreover, any change that affects the length of a line will usually entail resetting the remainder of its paragraph. Although it is a simple matter to call for inserting, deleting, or changing a word here and there, the consequent expenses can mount rapidly, and any such editing should have been completed before the manuscript was released for typesetting. A writer has no justification for releasing a manuscript that he is not willing to see printed as it stands. Proofreading is for correcting genuine errors, not for polishing a prematurely released manuscript.

When the annotated manuscript reaches the printer, his ultimate job is to prepare solid metallic plates for the presses that will print the actual copies. Since solid plates are unalterable for all practical purposes, however, all schemes for preparing the plates include an intermediate stage in which errors can be more readily corrected. (It may be debatable whether printing practices arose historically with this rationale, but the net result is essentially the same as if they had.)

We shall not attempt an exhaustive treatment of all currently used typesetting schemes. For concreteness, we shall base the discussion on linotype and monotype, which are still far more common than any others. But it should be borne in mind that essential features, such as a correctable intermediate stage, the complications of justifying (alining both ends of) the lines, and the inherent inefficiency of making corrections at widely scattered places, will all be shared by any system that might eventually replace the present standard ones.

Plain text (and as much mathematics as possible) is set by a keyboard machine. As the operator punches the keys, the machine automatically casts fresh, new type in justified lines*. Justification is accomplished by varying the spaces between words, and if necessary, between letters as well. Linotype casts a solid line of type that must be completely replaced if it contains an error, whereas monotype casts individual blocks for each letter and space. Although both machines are operated from a keyboard, the operator must be considerably more skilled than a typist, since he must control not only capitals and lower case letters, but also type font (bold, italic, small capital, as well as roman), type size, and any special characters (Greek alphabet or the like). He must also terminate each line at a length that can be justified with neither undue crowding nor extreme spacing, a rather complex job because the various letters have different widths. Moreover, in technical work, the keyboard (at least for monotype) may be varied from one job to another in order to accommodate various unusual symbols.

The lines of freshly cast metallic type are delivered from the machine into long trays, called "galley trays." Any necessary hand-set lines are inserted in their proper locations, and the galley trays then constitute

---

* Monotype actually prepares first a punched paper tape that is later fed to a completely automatic casting machine. The net result is the same as if the keyboard machine had cast the type.

the intermediate, correctable form, necessary in any scheme for making press plates. Although the galley type is correctable, it is in no sense a "rough draft"; it is the very type from which the plates, and hence the book, will be made. It will not be reset, in any practical sense, except as may be necessary to correct errors.

At this point, the printer takes an impression off each galley tray to produce what is known as a "galley proof." Since the type fits rather loosely in the trays, the impression is taken on thin, flexible paper, using a rather soft rubber roller. The alinement may be imperfect, and the impression is not as clean and sharp as it will later be, but the essentials are perfectly clear.

The printer (or his proofreader) then scans the galley proofs for broken letters, misspellings, wrong type fonts, or other obvious errors. In general, if a questionable item is not clearly wrong, he will assume that the author will automatically check it. Occasionally, a borderline situation may prompt him to call the author's attention to an item with a "query" written in the margin. He should be accorded the courtesy of an answer to each query. All he wants is a specific decision; there is no need to write him an essay on the matter.

The galley proofs are then sent to the author, who is expected to find all remaining errors and to indicate how they should be corrected. Since expensive equipment is being held out of use during this time, the author should either give the proofs his immediate attention or notify the publisher that this is impossible.

Each necessary correction must be given a mark in the margin of the galley proof: the printer looks in the margins for his instructions, and he may overlook an error that is marked only in the text. Corrections are best indicated by a more or less standard code, which is summarized in the table printed on pages 198-200. Essentially, the code consists of a set of abbreviated directions that are to be written in the nearer margin, beside the line to which they refer, and a set of corresponding marks to be written in the text to show the exact location of the error*. Marks within the text are thereby confined to a bare minimum for utmost clarity. The code is not completely standard, but variations within one country are minor. (The British system differs from ours primarily in using a λ-like symbol to indicate insertions.)

Because every typesetter is thoroughly accustomed to these proofreader's marks, they usually constitute the clearest, as well as the briefest, way of specifying corrections, and on that account, are well worth learning. Occasionally, an author will not be sure that he has made his wishes entirely clear, and he should then circle the characters to be corrected and write "To read: . . ." followed by the correct version, clearly hand-printed in ink, together with all necessary pencil markings to show type styles, special symbols, and sub- or superscripts. If there is not room for clear directions, a clean sheet of paper with the correct version can be pasted to the margin (and then folded face down over the galley proof to minimize the danger of its being torn). A little plain English is also not amiss when necessary, but there is no need to provide anything more than clear directions.

----

* If many errors occur in one line, the marginal notes should be written horizontally in the same order as that in which the errors occur. The different notes should then be separated by vertical slashes.

Never under any circumstances cut the proof sheets apart. Each one has a code at the top to identify the tray from which it came. If this code becomes separated from a section of proof, the corresponding blocks of type become very difficult to locate.

Remember that all corrections and changes marked on the galley will be made essentially by hand. Even though the corrected lines may be set on a machine, the material is not continuous text, and it must be inserted by hand into the proper positions in the galley trays. Correction by any method is inherently more time-consuming and less efficient than setting plain, continuous text. Because publishers have had much experience with extensive unnecessary resetting, it has become customary to charge the author directly for excessive revisions (but not for correction of printer's errors).

As long as the author confines himself to correction of genuine errors (his own or others') and resists the natural tendency to polish a work that he has not read for some time, he need not fear that his corrections will be excessive. Even an occasional revision of a particularly glaring ineptitude will not be serious, but such revisions should be made only when they are really important. Recall that the lines of type are justified by varying the word spaces, and that resetting the succeeding lines of the paragraph can be avoided if the revisions are arranged to leave the length of the line (or set of neighboring lines) essentially unchanged.

If material must be added or deleted, the cost will be minimized if it consists of whole paragraphs (or, next best, of new endings for old paragraphs). In book publishing, added paragraphs are not strictly corrections; they can be treated more like additional manuscript. In journal publishing, such material is more of a nuisance because the author sees only the first galley proofs; it is sometimes labelled "Note added in proof" to indicate that the author has not had an opportunity to proofread it.

When the author has finished checking the galley proofs, he sends one copy of the proofs *and the manuscript* to the publisher, who usually has his own proofreaders check them over, primarily for errors such as type layout, which an author might not notice. The publisher then sends the proofs back to the printer, who proceeds to correct the type in the galley trays. It is important for the author to return *all* material (except duplicates), because the manuscript and proofs are the only detailed records of the project, and much time and trouble can be saved by keeping them together.

If the work is a journal article, the author's job is completed when he returns the manuscript and first galley proofs. All subsequent work will be done by the editorial staff of the journal.

In book publishing, it is customary to make a second set of proofs from the corrected galley trays if a large number of corrections were made on the first proofs. These second galley proofs are likewise checked by the printer and sent to the author. The presumption is that few if any errors now remain in the type, and if the author originally submitted a clear, well polished manuscript, these second proofs may not even be necessary. If they are, it is assumed (unless otherwise arranged between the author and publisher) that the second set of corrections will make the type as nearly perfect as is humanly possible. The author, indeed, has then had two chances to find errors, and there would seem to be little need to give him a third. Moreover, it is widely recognized that too much correcting can easily introduce more errors than it removes.

At this stage the compositor assembles the type into page forms, which become the mold from which the press plates will be made. Not only must the compositor arrange any footnotes, tables, or figures properly, but he must also insert type for page numbers, multiple footnote references, and page headings. The consecutive pages of text must also be properly arranged in different positions, so that when the printed sheets are folded, interleaved, bound, and cut, the pages will appear in their proper order. Finally, the type itself (which has been comparatively "loose" up to this point) must be mechanically alined, leveled, and locked firmly into position.

Naturally, this work, too, must be adequately checked. The printer takes "page proofs" from the forms and again checks for broken type, improperly depressed space-blocks, and any other obvious errors. The page proofs are then sent to the author for his final approval. The presumption is that he will find virtually nothing to criticize. A few errors may be found, however.

In checking the page proofs, it behooves the author to consider very carefully the risks of requesting further corrections. Because so much more work must now be undone, a correction has become even more expensive. Moreover, the page-proof stage is very nearly a point of diminishing returns: previously locked type tends to stick together, and the page forms, with their locking devices, are not so well adapted as the galley trays to lifting out lines of type for correcting. In consequence, requesting a correction entails a danger of introducing as many errors as will be rectified. Printers are human too.

Of course corrections are still possible, and if they are truly important, there is no choice but to request them. At the very least, an author should feel a sense of shame if the error is one that was present on the galley proofs. Any error that increases the length of a page, or that otherwise rearranges material on more than a few pages, is a near-disaster for all concerned.

Finally, the author returns the page proofs to the publisher, and his job is completed. If any further errors remain after the press plates have been made, about the only way of correcting them is to arrange for publishing an errata sheet — or wait and hope for the chance to print a second edition.

PROOFREADERS' MARKS

PROOFREADERS' MARKS

	In Margin	*In Text*

REMOVE

Delete; take out completely*   *dele* or *dele* or *of*   / or ⸺

Close up; NO space

Delete and close up

Decrease space (between words)

SUBSTITUTE or INSERT

  —WORDS

Substitute or insert a word (print:)   **word** or **word#**   — or ∧

Insert material skipped   *omission* [1,2..]   ∧

Insert new material, not in MS   *insert* [1,2...]   ∧

    In these 2 cases, print (or type and paste) material

      in margin; label it *omitted* or *insert* (1,2...).

  —LETTERS

Substitute or insert capital letter   P   / or ∧

Lower case, "small" letter (print:)   p   / or ∧

  — joined to following word   p   / or ∧

  — joined at end of word   p   / or ∧

Change capital(s) to lower case   *l.c.* or *l.c.//...*   / or ///...

Change lower case to capital(s)   *cap.* or *caps.*   / or ≡

Substitute or insert subscript   ∧   / or ∧

  "   "   "   superscript   ∨   / or ∧

  —PUNCTUATION (Note the extra marks to attract attention.)

Period   ⊙   / or ∧

Comma   ⌃ or ,/   / or ∧

Apostrophe   ∨   / or ∧

Begin quotes   ⟨⟨   / or ∧

End quotes   ⟩⟩   / or ∧

Hyphen   -/ or =/   / or ∧

Dash (1 em long)   1/m   / or ∧

Colon   :/   / or ∧

Semicolon   ;/   / or ∧

Paren(s)   (/)   / / or ∧ ∧

Bracket(s)   [/]   / / or ∧ ∧

*The deletion symbol (a hasty dl?) varies greatly; be sure, however,
to keep it distinct from ⸮ , the turn over symbol.*

| | *In Margin* | *In Text* |

REARRANGE

	In Margin	*In Text*
Transpose; reverse order of items	*tr.*	⌒ or ⌒
Insert space (between words)	#	∧
Intersentence space (em quad)	□	∧
Center at middle of line	*center*	⟨ ∧ ⟩
Start new paragraph	¶	∧
Suppress paragraph	No ¶	

IGNORE (Try never to use this!)

| Leave as is; ignore correction | *stet* | .... |

TYPE STYLES

Letter(s) from wrong font	*w. f.*	═ or *O*
(Use only when the correct size or style is obvious)		
Roman (ordinary) type	*rom.*	◯
CAPITALS (roman)	*caps.*	───
SMALL CAPITALS	*sm. caps.*	═══
Italic type	*ital.*	───
Bold face type	*b.f.*	⌇⌇⌇
Bold face italic type	*b.f. ital.*	∿∿
ITALIC CAPITALS	*ital. caps.*	═══
BOLD FACE CAPITALS	*b.f. caps.*	≈≈≈
BOLD FACE ITALIC CAPITALS	*b.f. ital. caps.*	∿∿∿

(THESE UNDERLININGS MAY BE USED IN MANUSCRIPTS, AS WELL;
UNDER TYPED CAPITALS, THE BOTTOM 3 UNDERLINES USUALLY
MAY BE OMITTED.)

MECHANICAL IMPERFECTIONS

Replace broken letter	+ or ✕ or ⊕	/ or *O*
Push down spacer block	⊥ or ⊥	/ or *O*
Equalize word spacings	*eq.* #	⌄ ⌄ ⌄
Aline crooked word(s)	═ or *aline*	∧ ∧ ──
Turn over inverted letter	?	/ or ◯
Move word(s) left or right	⌐ or ⌐	⌐ or ⌐
Move word(s) up or down	⌐ or ⌐	⌐ or ⌐
Aline ends of lines	‖	(none)
Straighten crooked lines	≋	(none)
Space out 2 lines*	*lead >* or *ld. >*	(none)
Decrease interline space	*< d. lead* or *ld. >*	(none)

*Here, lead *refers to metal strips used as line spacers.*

A CORRECTED PROOFSHEET

TYPOGRAPHICAL ERRORS.

It does not appear that the earliest printers had any method of correcting errors before the form was on the press, The learned The learned correctors of the first two centuries of printing were not proof-readers in our sense, they were rather what we should term office editors. Their labors were chiefly to see that the proof corresponded to the copy, but that the printed page was correct in its latinity, that the words were there, and that the sense was right. They cared but little about orthography, bad letters or purely printers errors, and when the text seemed to them wrong they consulted fresh authorities or altered it on their own responsibility. Good proofs in the modern sense, were impossible until professional readers were employed, men who had first a printer's education, and then spent many years in the correction of proof. The orthography of English, which for the past century has undergone little change, was very fluctuating until after the publication of Johnson's Dictionary, and capitals, which have been used with considerable regularity for the past 80 years, were previously used on the miss or hit plan. The approach to regularity, so far as we have, may be attributed to the growth of a class of professional proof-readers, and it is to them that we owe the correctness of modern printing. More errors have been found in the Bible than in any other one work. For many generations it was frequently the case that Bibles were brought out stealthily, from fear of governmental interference. They were frequently printed from imperfect texts, and were often modified to meet the views of those who publised them. The story is related that a certain woman in Germany, who was the wife of a printer, and had become disgusted with the continual assertions of the superiority of man over woman which she had heard, hurried into the composing room

INDEX

Abbreviations, 55-57, 177
  coining of, 56
  grammatical, 34
  punctuation of, 151
Absolute construction, 37, 136
Abstract, 67
Abstract nouns, 109
Accounting, grammatical closure,
  31-33
Active voice, 38, 110
  advantages of, 38, 111
Address (vocative), 123
Adjectives, 125-127
  as nouns, 35
  as verb complements, 112
  parallel, 163
Adverb, 125-127
  conjunctive, 167, 175
  parallel, 163
  relative, 132
Adverbial clauses, 133
Affect, 178
Agreement of subject and verb,
  37
Alliteration, 80-81
Allusion, 45, 54, 174
Alternate readings, 35, 49, 172
Ambiguity, grammatical, 35-36
  in vocabulary, 49-52, 172
Analogy, 81
Antecedent of pronoun, 58, 120
Apologies, 103
Apostrophe, 154
Apparently ungrammatical
  constructions, 37
Appendixes, 69, 97
Applications (examples), 71,
  101, 104

Appositive, 136
  punctuation of, 167
  simplification with, 34
Architecture, 71-73, 89-94
Arrangement of message, 94-98,
  102
Articles *(a, an, the),* 109
Asides, 55, 178
Auxiliary verbs, 112-119
Balance (parallelism), 39, 134,
  139
Balanced sentence, 139
Beginning of a paper, 67, 74, 96,
  102
Brackets (in quotations), 156
Brevity, 73-74, 104
Cards, use of, 95
Causal conjunctions, 123
Checking plans, 96
Classes (linguistic), 141
Clause, 131-133
  nonrestrictive ("dispensible"),
    59, 165
  restrictive, 59, 165
Closing a paper, 69, 97
Closure, grammatical, 31-33
Coined words, 59
Colloquialisms, 58, 155
Colon, 158
Comma, 157-167
  after introductory material,
    159
  for interruptions, 164-167
  in a series, 159-161
  in compound predicates, 158
  in compound sentences, 157
Comments, in scientific writing,
  77

201

Comparative (of adjectives and adverbs), 126
Comparison, completion of, 127
Complement (of a verb)
objective, 112
subjective, 111
Compositor, 195
Compound sentence, 137, 157
Compound verbs, 112-119
splitting of, 32
Compound words, 152
Conciseness, 74, 104
Conclusions, 69, 97
Concrete nouns, 109
Conditional grammatic forms, 55, 82, 104, 116
Conjunction, 123
Conjunctive adverbs, 167, 175
Connotations, 45, 54, 174
Constituent, immediate (linguistic), 141
Contractions, 56
Danger signals, 174-180
Dangling modifiers, 37, 130
Dashes, 167
Deadlines, contending with, 104
Definitions, value to reader, 76, 102, 104
Demonstrative pronouns, 121
Denials, 97
Diagnosis, 173
Dictionary, value of, 50
Digressions, 69, 96
Dispensible clause, 59, 165
Division of words, 152
Double negatives, 177
Double-edged modifier, 36
Draft, 91
Durative form of verb, 114
Editorial services, 171, 188
limitations on, 90
Editorial *we*, 39, 121
Effect, 178
Elegance, 54, 78
Eliminating structure words, 34, 176

Ellipsis (in quotations), 156
Elliptic constructions, 34
Emphasis, 97
in speech, 20
in writing, 52-54, 97
relative, 73, 94
Evolution of language, 107
Examples, value to reader, 71, 101, 104
Excessive punctuation, 162, 180
Experimenting, 92
Explanations, "elementary", 71, 104
Expletive, 136
Expository writing, 10
Figures of speech, 54, 81-83
Flowing style, 26
Footnotes, in MS, 186
Former, latter, 57, 177
Function words (linguistics), 141
Functionless phrases, 22, 43-45, 178
Galley proofs, 191-194
Generalities,
as main theme, **71**
immediately particularized, 46-47, **178**
philosophical, 54, 104
Gerunds, 130
Glancing back (symptom), 52, 57, 172
Grammar, 107-145
and meaning, 107
as metalanguage, 26, 142
craftsmanship required, 26-29, 108, 173
in speech, 21, 27
value of, 26, 107-109
viewed functionally, 143-145
Grammatical closure, 31-33
Habits, from speech, 27, 42, 45, 49, 89
Has as, 175
Hasty phrasing, 45-49
Have, as auxiliary verb, **113**

Hinting, 45, 54, 174
Historical present tense, 114
Homographs, 49
However, 175
Humor, 54
Hyphen, 152-154, 177
Idiom and prepositions, 50, 123
Illogical phrases, 37, 51
Illustrations (examples), value, 71, 101, 104
Imagery, 54, 81-83
Immediate constituent (linguistics), 141
Imperative (mood of verb), 116
Implication, 45, 54, 97, 174
In that, 179
Incomplete grammatical forms, 34
Indefinite pronouns, 39, 120, 177
Index cards, 95
Indicative (mood of verb), 116
Indirect object, 135
Infinitive, 128
    phrases, 129
    splitting, 32
Inflection of pronouns, 121
Influence of writings, 11, 84
Insertions, 29
    dangers of, 174
    in galley proof, 193
Inspiration of readers, 11, 84
Interjection, 123
Interrogative pronouns, 120
Interruptions, 30-32
    and ease of reading, 28
    punctuation of, 164-168
Introduction, 67, 74, 96, 102
Introductory modifiers, 159
Italic type, 53, 146
Jargon, 58, 76
Juncture, 140
Language, 19, 107, 140
    evolution of, 107
    one-dimensionality, 92
    written *vs* spoken, 19-25, 140
Latin abbreviations, 56

Latter, former, 57, 177
Linear (serial) property of language, 92
Linguistics, structural, 140-143
Literary writing, 10
Manuscript preparation, 183-189
Mathematics, typesetting of, 185
Meaning, and ambiguous words, 49-52
    and grammar, 107
Metaphor, 54, 81-83
Mode of a verb, 116-120
Modifier, 125-127
    dangling, 37, 130
    double-edged, 36
    grammar of, 125-127
    overuse, 45-48, 52, 173-174
    parallel, 163
    preliminary, 159
    restrictive, nonrestrictive, 165-166
    shortening of, 33
Mood of a verb, 116-120
    subjunctive, value of, 55, 82, 104
Morpheme, 140
Negative, double, 177
Nominative absolute, 37, 136
Nonrestrictive clause, etc., 59, 165
Nonverbal signals, 19
Notes, 92, 95
Notebooks, 96
Nouns, abstract and concrete, 109
    used as adjectives, 35, 36, 177
Object, 110, 123
    indirect, 135
    of a preposition, 123
    of a verbal, 129, 130
Objective complement, 112
Objectivity, 77-78
    and editorial *we*, 39
One-dimensionality of language, 92

Opening paragraphs, 67, 74, 96, 102
Order of words, and meaning, 35, 107
Organization, 55, 71, 89-106
Outlining, 48, 91-98
Overzealousness, 48, 52
Pace, 73-75, 104
Page proofs, 195
Pallid prose, 78
Paragraphing, 40, 98-102
Parallel modifiers, 163
Parallelism, 39, 134, 139
Parentheses, 167
Participle, 129
  dangling, 37, 130
  in absolute construction, 37, 136
  phrases, 130
Particle, 128
Parts of speech, 122
  adjectives and adverbs, 125-127
  conjunctions, 123
  interjections, 123
  nouns, 109
  prepositions, 123
  pronouns, 120-122
  verbs, 109, 128, 129
Passive voice, 38, 110
  weakness, complexity of, 38, 111
Pauses and punctuation, 148
Perfect tenses, 113, 129
Period (punctuation), 151
Periodic sentence, 139
Person, 109, 120
Personal pronouns, 121
Personality, in scientific writing, 78
Philosophical asides, 55, 104
Phoneme, 140
Phrase, 128
  infinitive, 129
  participial, 130

prepositional, 128
Planning, 89-106
Possessives, formation, 154
Precision, of word-choice, 42-60
  overdone, 52
  verbose, 46
Preliminary modifiers, 159
Preposition, 123
  choice of, 50, 123, 176
  elimination of, 33, 176
  phrases, 128
Pressure, writing under, 104
Printing procedures, 183-196
Progressive (verb form), 114
Pronouns, 120-122
  case determination, 122
  danger in, 58
  demonstrative, 121
  indefinite, 39, 120
  interrogative, 120
  personal, 121
  reflexive, 111
  relative, 23, 121, 132
Proofreading, of manuscript, 187-189
  of galley proofs, 191-194, 198
  of page proofs, 195
Pruning, of sentences, 33-35
Publication procedures, 183-196
Punctuation, 146-169
  conventionality, 23, 147, 149
  economizing, 162
  excessive, 28, 180
  modern purpose, 22, 149
  origin, 146
  quotations, 155-156
  tabular summary, 169
  unrelated to pauses, 148
  within sentences, 157-168
Purple prose, 54, 78
Qualifications, 29
Readers, 17-25, 61-85
  interest, 62-65
  position of, 17-25, 61
  understanding, 65-67

Reading and listening, 19-22
Redundancy, 33, 46, 59
    value of, 53, 73-74, 97
Referent (of a pronoun), 120
Reflexive pronoun, 111
Relative adverbs, 132
Relative pronouns, 23, 121, 132
Repetition, 51, 53
    imprecise, 51
    intentional, 53, 97
Rereading (retracing), symptom,
    52, 57, 172
Restrictive clause, 59, 165
Rewriting, 170-182
Rhythm, 39, 79
Scientific objectivity, 77
Scientific writing, 11, 77
Semicolon, 158, 161
Sentence, 75, 137-140
    balanced, 139
    complex, compound, 137
    core of, 109
    periodic, 139
    shortening of, 33, 104
    topic, 100
Serial property of language, 92
Shall and will, 112, 117
Shift, of subject or argument, 69,
    96
Shortening sentences, 33, 104
Shuffle draft, 92-98
Simile, 81-83
Simplifying devices, 31, 34, 38
So that, 175
Solecism, 51
Sound, in writing, 79-81
Special terms, choosing, 56, 95
Speech, difference from writing,
    18-24
    habits from, 27, 42, 45, 49, 89
    nonverbal signals in, 19
Spirit of grammar, 26, 108, 173
Split (infinitives, etc.), 32
Square brackets, 156
Squinting modifiers, 36
Starting to write, 90, 102

Straw man, 103
Stress (linguistics), 140
    emphasis, 52, 97
    unconscious (danger in), 24,
    172
Strings of similar words, 36, 176,
    177
Structural linguistics, 140
Structure of a work, 67-78,
    89-106
Structure words (linguistics),
    141
Style, 26, 77-83
Subject, of a verb, 109
Subjective complement, 111
Subjectivity, 77-78
Subjunctive mood, 116
    value of, 55, 82, 104
Substantive (grammar), 123
Such, 177
Sufficiently that, 176
Suggesting ideas, 45, 54, 174
Summaries, 69, 97
Superlative, 126
Syllable division, 152
Technical terms, 56, 59, 76, 102,
    104
Technical writing, 11, 77
Tense, 112-116
Terminology, grammatical, 26,
    109-140
    special, 56, 95
    technical, 59, 76, 104
That and which, 23, 59, 174
Thesaurus, 50
Tone, stylistic, 78
    in linguistics, 140
Topic sentence, 100
Transitive verbs, 110
Troubleshooting, 170-181
Typesetting practices, 183-196
    and mathematics, 185-186
Underlining codes, 199
Understanding, leading reader to,
    65-71
Ungrammatical forms, 27, 37

Uninformative phrases, 22, 43-45, 178
Unity, 55, 71-73
Vacuous constructions, 22, 43-45, 178
Vagueness, 45
Verb, 109-120
  active and passive, 38, 110
  durative form, 114
  finite, 109
  infinitives, 128
  moods, 116-120
  participles, 129-131
  progressive form, 114
  subject, object, complement of, 109-112, 135
  tenses, 112-116
  transitive, intransitive, 110
  voice, 38, 110
Verbal, 128

Verbosity, 33, 43-49, 74
Vocabularly, level of, 51, 76, 104
  precision of, 42-60
Vocative (direct address), 123
Voice (of verb form), 38, 110
  active preferable, 38, 111
Voice of writer, 78-81
We, editorial, 39, 121
When, 60, 174
Where, 60, 174
Which and *that*, 23, 59, 174
While, 60, 174
Will and *shall*, 112, 117
Word classes (linguistic), 141
  functional, 144-145
Word position, 35, 107
  emphasis by, 52
Word punctuation, 151-155
Writer's voice, 78-81